perennial

twila paris

with starla paris novak
illustrated by angie paris

perennial

meditations
for the
seasons of life

ZondervanPublishingHouse
Grand Rapids, Michigan

A Division of HarperCollinsPublishers

Perennial
Text copyright © 1998 by Twila Paris
Illustrations copyright © 1998 by Angie Paris

Requests for information should be addressed to:

ZondervanPublishingHouse
Grand Rapids, Michigan 49530

ISBN: 0-310-21622-2

This edition printed on acid-free paper and meets the American National Standards Institute Z39.48 standard.

Interior design by Sherri L. Hoffman

Printed in the United States of America

98 99 00 01 02 03 04 /❖ DC/ 10 9 8 7 6 5 4 3 2 1

For Mom and Dad

My dad is my pastor, and as I wrote this book, I began to realize how often I was quoting him. So many of the significant memories in my life involve a few wise words from my father. He always understood that every father is the pastor of his family, whatever his broader vocation may be, and at home, he consistently lived the same principles he taught on Sunday.

My mother's instruction, though less verbal, was just as powerful. Her gentle spirit, patience, and humility spoke eloquently of her deep commitment to God and to her family.

Though my parents spent countless hours in ministry to others, my brother and sisters and I never sensed anything less than their complete attention to even our smallest needs. This book is dedicated to Mom and Dad with gratitude for a Christlike example and a home filled with love.

contents

acknowledgments

Our heartfelt thanks to Mike Novak, Jack Wright, Oren Paris III, Jana Hoober, Ted and Snook Sebaugh, Cari Cox, Ann Spangler, Norman Miller, Meg Hinton, Mary Jay, and Jayne Farrell. We so appreciate your valuable contributions to this book.

perennial

A couple of years ago we bought a new (old) home and inherited a lovely garden—which, I think, must be something like a bachelor inheriting a small child. Still, with a lot of help, I've actually taken a few baby steps toward becoming a gardener. However, I've taken a giant leap toward appreciating the beauty of a well-planned and well-implemented garden. Of course, we plant a few annuals each spring, but I am especially enthralled with the perennials—those wonderful, generous plants that reappear and bloom every year with little or no effort on my part.

Just like the flowers in my garden and like certain classic hymns, there are passages of Scripture, principles of faith, and potent memories that blossom over and over again at just the right time to recreate God's miracle of grace in my heart. These perennial moments and messages resurface from time to time and always seem to do God's work in me in a fresh way. I've collected them here in the hope that they may reawaken or germinate truths God has planted in your heart.

My sister Starla has helped me with the writing of this project. She is the true gardener in our family, and I am learning a lot from her as we go along. Throughout this book, among the parables and principles, we have scattered a few of our favorite tidbits from the physical garden—just for your enjoyment. My youngest sister Angie is an artist, and all the illustrations are hers.

My sisters are my best girlfriends, and when we get together, whether just the three of us or with other friends, several things automatically happen. We talk about spiritual things; we talk about practical things. We share personal news and general news. Often we laugh—sometimes we cry. And somebody always ends up learning something from someone else.

Think of this book as a place you can visit. It's not necessarily meant to be read straight through or even "a page a day." Open the book—start anywhere you like and read as long as you like. We simply hope each time you come you take away at least one thing to think about, pray about, or try in your kitchen. And we pray that this book will always provide a moment of rest and encouragement in your day.

You may even be inspired to keep and share a record of the blossoms in your own "perennial garden." I believe it will cause your faith to grow—as it has mine. Happy gardening!

Love,

Twila

spring

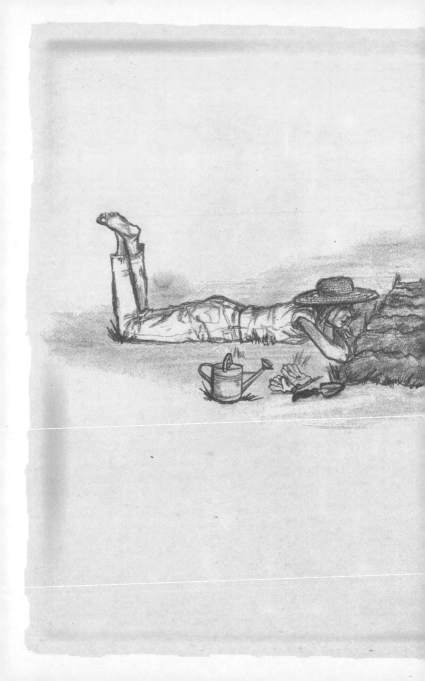

Spring carries with it a freshness that invigorates the body and spirit. In the garden, spring is a time of great activity and expectation. The winter is past, and the gardener longs to be about the art of growing. The soil, which has been prepared during the autumn and winter, awaits the new seeds and seedlings. Spring garden activities include sowing, transplanting, watering, and waiting. Gardeners often survey the newly planted garden, hoping to catch a glimpse of fresh sprouts peeking up through the soil. The birth of a garden and the resurgence of perennials is a lesson in the pure joy of new life emerging from what was once a cold, hard piece of earth. It is very much like the daily renewal in the heart of a child of God as the seeds He has planted are allowed to take root, sprout, and spread.

Quiet Time

But I will sing of your strength, in the morning I will sing of your love; for you are my fortress, my refuge in times of trouble. O my Strength, I sing praise to you; you, O God, are my fortress, my loving God.

PSALM 59:16–17

When we were very young, our dad impressed upon all of us the importance of a morning quiet time. He has remained a consistent, faithful example of spending this time alone with the Lord. Daybreak often found him seated at the dining room table reading his Bible and writing in his journal. When the weather permitted, I remember seeing him pace around the backyard, praying and singing worship songs to the Lord. Sometimes he sang out loud, never caring what the neighbors thought. I've certainly had my share of mornings when I hit the ground running—going through the whole day without spending a quiet time with the Lord. But those are never the best days. Of course, God's grace is there, but whenever I've allowed too many of those days into my life, it results in a tendency to rely on my own strength, which is always bad news.

King David had a schedule that would rival most. He was the ruler of a large nation, a husband, father, and close friend to many, yet he still found time to be alone with God. He understood the importance of a regular time, preferably in the morning, spent with the Lord. He knew that he relied on the daily wisdom he received from the Lord to make his way straight.

Whether praising God for His magnificent splendor or agonizing over an enemy's onslaught, David was in constant communication with God.

It is to our spiritual advantage to mirror this approach in our quiet times. Our days are unpredictable; sometimes happiness awaits, sometimes trouble. Busy days and hectic schedules only reinforce the need for a quiet time in the presence of the Lord. It is helpful to "make an appointment" with the Lord each morning before our day begins. He will always be on time, and He is ready to lovingly speak with us.

My Lips Will Praise You

My lips will praise You for You are holy
My voice will ever rise before Your throne
My heart will love You for You are lovely
And You have called me to become Your own

I am Your own, and I will worship You alone
I am Your own, I am Your child
I am Your own, and I will worship at Your throne
I am Your own, and I will love You

My lips will praise You for You are holy
My voice will ever rise before Your throne
My heart will love You for You are lovely
And You have called me to become Your own

"My Lips Will Praise You," originally recorded on "Perennial—Songs for the Seasons of Life" (Sparrow Records) © 1988 Ariose Music/Mountain Spring Music—ASCAP.

The planting of morning glories is a well-loved tradition in this country. My dad fondly remembers his childhood custom of planting morning glories every spring with my grandmother. "They were so easy to grow!" He loved greeting each morning with them and watching their sweet blooms climb the trellis my grandpa had made. When you're ready to plant your morning glories, "nick" each seed and soak them in water overnight before planting them.

God's Comfort

Praise be to the God and Father of our Lord Jesus Christ, the Father of compassion and the God of all comfort, who comforts us in all our troubles, so that we can comfort those in any trouble with the comfort we ourselves have received from God. For just as the sufferings of Christ flow over into our lives, so also through Christ our comfort overflows.

2 CORINTHIANS 1:3–5

A very good friend of mine has what I call a "healing personality." If I'm hurting, it makes me feel better just to be around her. She somehow seems to know what to say and what not to say.

I used to wonder why my friend was so good at comforting others. Then I heard the stories of how she had suffered early in her life, and I realized that she understands the pain of those around her. But simply having suffered is not enough. Suffering makes some people bitter. My friend knows how to offer comfort, because in her brokenness she reached out to her Father and allowed Him to comfort her. If you're hurting today, go to God for comfort. If you are willing, He will change your sorrow into a healing balm that you can turn and pour out on those around you.

It's no wonder the hymn writer referred to Christ as the "Lily of the Valley." These richly scented perennials, probably the most fragrant of all perennials, have long been the symbol of purity of heart.

Thanks in All Things

Be joyful always; pray continually; give thanks in all circum-
stances, for this is God's will for you in Christ Jesus.

1 THESSALONIANS 5:16–18

*F*or the twelve years we've been married, my husband, Jack,
has suffered much of the time from a combination of several health problems. Some days have been better than others,
but overall our life has been very unpredictable. At one point, we
almost completely stopped making plans to do anything
together, because we were so rarely able to follow through.

I've heard it said that trials encountered by married couples
will either pull them apart or bring them closer together. Jack and
I love one another very deeply and believe that we have truly
been brought closer together by the circumstances we have faced.
And Jack's strength is growing as he continues to learn to pace
himself and rest in the Lord. Even so, the disappointments, challenges, and fears that can accompany chronic illness have
affected us both as a couple and individually. I personally struggled a great deal with self-pity, especially at first. I've heard my
father say that self-pity is the opposite of gratefulness, and I
believe he is right. Thanksgiving will rule in our hearts and minds
if we are choosing to meditate on the mercy and goodness of God,
on His faithfulness and blessings to us, and on who He is.

Early on, I had begun to recognize that the difficult circumstances in my life were influencing my ministry in a positive way.
Without thinking about it, I was naturally writing songs that
were encouraging and comforting to others who were facing

their own unrealized dreams. However, I had a hard time remembering to be grateful for this fact, and after a while almost began to resent it. I wanted someone else to have a turn at writing those songs. Then I could write the songs about the fun aspects of the Christian life.

But the Spirit of God persevered in my heart, and I eventually did learn to find comfort in the fact that some good could result from the path God had allowed me to walk. Then one day, not so very long ago, I woke up and realized that I was receiving not only comfort, but actual joy and fulfillment from the knowledge that God was using my painful circumstances to bring hope and healing to others. I was finally able to give thanks for even this. It occurred to me that maybe this was a step in the direction of becoming a spiritual "grown-up."

Sweet Victory

Quietly You lead me to an open place
Hold me in the stillness till I see Your face
Waiting in the silence as You speak my name
Rising like an eagle I will fly

Sweet Victory over the enemy
Gentle Power, all I ever needed
Sweet Victory, I take it finally
Strength for running
It was a long time coming
Sweet Victory

In this place I rest in more than I can see
High above the turbulence You carry me
From deep in a full heart I will speak Your name
Rising like an eagle I will fly

Sweet Victory over the enemy
Gentle Power, all I ever needed
Sweet Victory, I take it finally
Strength for running
It was a long time coming

I held so tightly to my fear
There were so many sins repeated
But Your love has brought me here
And the Victory is sweet
Victory is sweet

Sweet Victory, the blood of Calvary
Gentle Power, all I ever needed
Sweet Victory, I take it finally
Strength for running
Sweet Victory

"Sweet Victory," originally recorded on "For Every Heart"
(Star Song Records) © 1988 Ariose Music/Mountain Spring
Music—ASCAP.

*C*reating and keeping a "gratefulness calendar" is a great way to record the faithfulness of the Lord in our daily lives. Our keeping track also serves as a history lesson for all the years yet to come — reminding us that the thoughts of the Lord are precious concerning us; they "outnumber the sand."

Say Something Nice

> Get rid of all bitterness, rage and anger, brawling and slander,
> along with every form of malice. Be kind and compassionate to
> one another, forgiving each other, just as in Christ God forgave
> you. Be imitators of God, therefore, as dearly loved children and
> live a life of love, just as Christ loved us and gave himself up for
> us as a fragrant offering and sacrifice to God.
>
> EPHESIANS 4:31–32; 5:1–2

One childhood memory most of us share is the movie *Bambi*. My favorite character was Thumper. Maybe it's because I can relate to his tendency to open his mouth, before he thought, and say the wrong thing. We can probably all quote along with him his mother's admonition, "If you can't say somethin' nice, don't say nothin' at all."

Being kind to one another is such a simple concept. It's one of the first Christian principles we teach our children. Yet we all know that even supposedly "mature" Christians who think deep theological thoughts can sometimes have great difficulty with just being kind. And if simple kindness is hard—what about forgiveness? Christ is our perfect example of kindness, compassion, and forgiveness; and God does not give us permission to leave these simple truths behind as we move on in our faith. If we have to remind ourselves every single morning to cultivate kindness, love, tenderheartedness, and forgiveness *today*, then let's do it. Because these things are important to God, they must also be important to us.

*I*f you're having a little trouble with unwelcome guests on your vegetable plants, you might want to plant some herbs and flowers in and around them. This will help encourage "beneficials," like ladybugs, to "move in" and flourish. Also, marigolds planted around the perimeter of your garden help deter rabbits.

Gracious Speech

Devote yourselves to prayer, being watchful and thankful. And pray for us, too, that God may open a door for our message, so that we may proclaim the mystery of Christ, for which I am in chains. Pray that I may proclaim it clearly, as I should. Be wise in the way you act toward outsiders; make the most of every opportunity. Let your conversation be always full of grace, seasoned with salt, so that you may know how to answer everyone.

COLOSSIANS 4:2–6

I have seen Christian brothers and sisters given the opportunity to speak in a public forum who made me feel honored to be associated with them. Others made me cringe, and I was almost embarrassed to be identified with them. I found myself hoping that not many people were listening. And I couldn't help wondering if the Lord felt the same way.

I believe there is never any reason to be obnoxious for Jesus. We do Him no service when our personalities repel others. It is gracious speech without compromise that attracts unbelievers to the message of truth and love.

Lord, please help me to always represent You in a way that truly reflects Your heart of love and mercy.

*C*rocuses, mentioned in Isaiah 35:1–2, are a variety of bulbs that include spring and fall blooming species. Crocus stigmas also produce saffron, an expensive spice, used to flavor many seafood and pasta dishes.

Who Are We Working For?

Whatever you do, work at it with all your heart, as working for the Lord, not for men, since you know that you will receive an inheritance from the Lord as a reward. It is the Lord Christ you are serving.

COLOSSIANS 3:23–24

When I was a teenager, I worked in my parents' Bible bookstore. Just the fact that it was my parents' store made me want to be sure I was always friendly, courteous, and helpful to everyone who came in. I was naturally aware that my attitude, demeanor, and performance would always reflect on my mom and dad.

If we, as Christians, would keep in mind Who we are really working for, then we would consistently stand out as the most productive, efficient segment of society. Verse 23 says, "whatever you do"—meaning whether you are doing homework for your math teacher, cooking dinner for your family, building cars on an assembly line, or performing heart surgery—you are called to do it as unto the Lord. Our work then becomes a very practical form of worship.

God's rewards are based on faithfulness, not on how important we perceive our job to be. Let's purpose in our hearts that we will glorify God in our work today—whatever we do.

Family Worship

May the words of my mouth and the meditation of my heart be pleasing in your sight, O LORD, my Rock and my Redeemer.

PSALM 19:14

When I was young we had family worship in the morning right after breakfast. At the end of our time together we would always close by praying aloud Psalm 19:14. As an adult I have an even greater appreciation for my dad's wisdom in choosing this particular verse. What a wonderful thing to commit your words and thoughts to the Lord each morning before you go out to face the challenges and opportunities of the day. And of course when the things we say and think are pleasing to God, the things we do are never far behind.

Watering your garden in the morning instead of the evening reduces the risk of disease by allowing your plants to fully dry in the warmth of the day. If your plants have a tendency to scorch, make sure to water only the soil, not the foliage. This will keep the plant dry and free from various molds and fungi.

We Seek His Face

The Lord is mighty, the Lord is holy
The Lord is present in this place
And we behold Him, we see His goodness
We know His mercy and His grace
We seek His face, we seek His Face

The Lord is risen, the Lord is coming
And all the earth shall sing His praise
And to behold Him in all His glory
In all His power and His grace
We seek His face, we seek His face

Alleluia, God is with us
Alleluia, Christ is coming
Alleluia, God is with us
Alleluia, Christ is coming

The Lord is mighty, the Lord is holy
The Lord is present in this place
The Lord is mighty, the Lord is holy
The Lord is present in this place
We seek His face

"We Seek His Face," originally recorded on "Perennial—Songs for the Seasons of Life" (Sparrow Records) © 1988 Ariose Music/Mountain Spring Music—ASCAP.

Spiritual Warfare

For our struggle is not against flesh and blood, but against the
rulers, against the authorities, against the powers of this dark world
and against the spiritual forces of evil in the heavenly realms.

EPHESIANS 6:12

As a little girl, Starla had an extremely vivid imagination. Our brother Oren was more practical but was a year younger, so he often followed her in whatever adventure she had planned for the day. Once, when they were three and four years old, they ran into the house from playing outside and announced that they had killed the Devil and buried him in the backyard. Evidently, they had actually been listening to the previous Sunday's teaching on the subject of spiritual warfare.

I was a few years older, and I had my doubts about the wisdom of interring the Prince of Darkness on our own property. Still, on the whole, it was a valiant effort, and I was mainly glad the outcome had not been reversed.

As adults, we know that our battles against Satan take place in the spiritual realm, yet we find out very quickly that the wounds can still be deep. The enemy of our souls is aggressively trying to take our very life. Often the most committed Christians and those in leadership suffer the greatest attacks because they are on the front lines.

Whether you are a baby Christian or have been given some degree of responsibility to lead, God is your source of strength, comfort, and protection. It is good to remember this, even when you're winning. None of us ever outgrows the need to run home to the Father when we have been overwhelmed by the struggle. If we honestly pour out our hurts and fears to Him, He will graciously bind up our wounds and equip us for future victories.

Although they love to munch on many garden delicacies, slugs avoid certain perennials including foxgloves and hardy begonias. This is great news for gardeners who love to avoid slugs!

The Warrior Is a Child

Lately I've been winning battles left and right
But even winners can get wounded in the fight
People say that I'm amazing, strong beyond my years
But they don't see inside of me
I'm hiding all the tears

They don't know that I go running home when I fall down
They don't know who picks me up when no one is around
I drop my sword and cry for just awhile
'Cause deep inside this armor the warrior is a child

Unafraid because His armor is the best
But even soldiers need a quiet place to rest
People say that I'm amazing, never face retreat
But they don't see the enemies
that lay me at His feet

They don't know that I go running home when I fall down
They don't know who picks me up when no one is around
I drop my sword and look up for a smile
'Cause deep inside this armor
The warrior is a child

True Friends

*Therefore encourage one another and build each
other up, just as in fact you are doing.*

1 THESSALONIANS 5:11

*O*ne day, several years ago, my friend Jayne called, with no
agenda but to encourage me. She told me how much my latest album had ministered to her and that she had actually bought
it to pass along to several friends. She had no way of knowing
that she had called at a particular moment when I especially
needed to hear just what she had to say. Her obedience to God
not only inspired a friend, but also the lyrics to a song.

We need one another for so many reasons in the body of
Christ. One very important reason is encouragement. None of us
can begin to count the times that we have been encouraged by
another member of the body of Christ, whether on a personal
level or in the sermon on Sunday morning. We can all remember
times when we felt so weak and tired that we were almost ready
to give up, and God spoke the exact words we needed to hear at
just the right moment through a faithful brother or sister.

The Father wants us to not only receive but also give encouragement on a regular basis—to go through the day speaking
words that build up those around us, to be sensitive and always
listening, so that we can offer specific and timely encouragement. If someone is on your mind today, go ahead and pick up
the phone or write a note. You may be the voice of God to a desperately weary heart.

Some days I feel like a failure
And I'd love to leave it all
I see no reason to go on
That's when you decide to call
Making it simple and clear
That's why your voice is so dear
My heart takes courage from hearing you say

You are a true friend
Pointing me to Him
Lifting my downcast eyes
Turning my wandering gaze to the sky
Proving your love again
You are a true friend

"True Friend" originally recorded on "For Every Heart" (Star Song Records) © 1988 Ariose Music/Mountain Spring Music—ASCAP.

When we entertain, I enjoy adding simple little touches throughout our home that say "welcome" to our company. One easy summer addition from the garden is fresh-cut flowers. Buds with stems that are too short for arranging in vases are perfect companions for floating candles in a variety of pretty little bowls of water. These brighten hallway tables and coffee tables and window ledges.

Good Soil

Then Jesus said to them, "Don't you understand this parable? How then
will you understand any parable? The farmer sows the word. Some
people are like seed along the path, where the word is sown. As soon as
they hear it, Satan comes and takes away the word that was sown in
them. Others, like seed sown on rocky places, hear the word and at
once receive it with joy. But since they have no root, they last only a
short time. When trouble or persecution comes because of the word,
they quickly fall away. Still others, like seed sown among thorns, hear
the word; but the worries of this life, the deceitfulness of wealth and the
desires for other things come in and choke the word, making it unfruit-
ful. Others, like seed sown on good soil, hear the word, accept it, and
produce a crop—thirty, sixty or even a hundred times what was sown."

MARK 4:13–20

*O*n more than one occasion I've found myself sitting in church
listening intently and thinking, *Oh, that's a great point; I hope*
"so-and-so" is listening! That's exactly what he needs to do.

It's so easy to hear a wonderful sermon and assume it's for
someone else, or to receive the truth, only to forget it twenty-
four hours later. There are many lies and distractions in the
world around us, and yet God says that our hearts should be a
place where His Word can take root and grow—like a green-
house where the seeds are nurtured and protected from predators and the environment. The choices we make ultimately
determine the quality of the soil in our hearts. Is the seed of

God's Word easily stolen or destroyed in your heart, or is your heart a safe place where the seeds can grow and produce a beautiful crop?

Saving seeds is an inexpensive way to grow your favorite vegetable varieties year after year. Fresh tomato seeds can be saved by placing them in a glass of water away from direct sunlight. The water should be stirred each day to encourage any remaining pulp to rise to the top so that it may be discarded. Continue adding clean water and removing the additional film at the top. After about five days, the clean seeds that have settled to the bottom should be removed and air dried. You can then place them in an envelope and store them in a dark drawer until seed-planting time in the spring.

The Heavens Declare

The heavens declare the glory of God; the skies proclaim the work of his hands. Day after day they pour forth speech; night after night they display knowledge. There is no speech or language where their voice is not heard. Their voice goes out into all the earth, their words to the ends of the world. In the heavens he has pitched a tent for the sun, which is like a bridegroom coming forth from his pavilion, like a champion rejoicing to run his course. It rises at one end of the heavens and makes its circuit to the other; nothing is hidden from its heat.

PSALM 19:1–6

I remember a sentence I prayed one evening a few years ago. "Lord, the sky was so beautiful today!" That night I thought to express verbally what happens in my heart, and probably yours, on a regular basis. God's creation shouts to us every day of His glory and awesome power. It also whispers of His love and peace. If we really are watching and listening, our response will always be one of spontaneous worship and gratitude.

Of course we should never make the common mistake of placing the creation higher than the Creator, but when nature is held in the proper prospective, it will continually call our attention to God.

You may have noticed that your multivitamin contains rose hips and/or raspberry leaves. Both of these natural additives contain calcium and vitamin E, which help keep our bones, skin, and teeth healthy.

Cycle of Giving

For from him and through him and to him are all things.
To him be the glory forever! Amen.

ROMANS 11:36

This verse has been a "life Scripture" for me. I believe it represents the appropriate cycle of giving between God and His children. Everything I have, everything I am or can be, comes from God. Any gifts or talents I have are given by Him, and He is the one whose plan and direction bring these gifts to their full potential. Naturally they should be returned to Him. All my time, abilities, and belongings should be used for His purposes. I should offer myself daily as a living sacrifice, not because I am so noble or such an exceptional saint, but simply because it's appropriate. If I do this, wonderful fruit will result in my life and in the Kingdom of God. And when it does, the glory should never be given to me, the vessel. It should always go to Him, the source and the continuance of all good things.

Every seed grows because of the loving care of the Lord. Water droplets evaporate and become clouds. Clouds produce rain. Rain falls to the earth and causes all living things to grow. The water cycle is a simple, yet amazing aspect of God's care for us.

Love Your Neighbor

"Teacher, which is the greatest commandment in the Law?" Jesus replied: "'Love the Lord your God with all your heart and with all your soul and with all your mind.' This is the first and greatest commandment. And the second is like it: 'Love your neighbor as yourself.' All the Law and the Prophets hang on these two commandments."

MATTHEW 22:36–40

Last summer one of Starla's friends grew a bumper crop of blueberries. She asked Starla and some other friends to come and pick all they could; otherwise they would go to waste. So she picked eight gallons of the most beautiful blueberries you've ever seen. Several pies and a couple of freezer bags later, we began asking what in the world she was going to do with all those blueberries!

A few days after that, a neighbor of Mike and Starla's, whom they waved at every day but had never formally met, surprised them with a huge bag of fresh corn on the cob, hand picked from her garden, already cleaned. She knew that their corn had not done well, so she walked the half mile up the road with her little daughter on her shoulders to deliver her gift. Starla offered to pay her and give her a ride home, but she wouldn't hear of it. "No, that's fine, I enjoyed the walk," she said.

As Starla put the fresh corn in the pressure cooker, a lingering question suddenly had an answer. She pulled out the largest bag of blueberries from her freezer and delivered them to her neighbor's door. That day we were clearly reminded of the importance of reaching out to show the love of God to people we often pass by but sometimes don't see.

The most important thing to God is relationship—His relationship with us and our relationships with one another. The thing that matters most to Him is that we love Him passionately with everything that is in us. Everything we do for Him should be motivated by that love. No ministry, not even evangelism, should be given a higher priority. If we busy ourselves telling others they can have a relationship with God, but do not take the time to develop our personal relationship with Him, then we have missed the whole point and we grieve the heart of our Father. True ministry is always an extension of true relationship with God. If we will simply love Him today, then loving one another and taking His love to the world will follow, and He will be pleased.

Starla loves to keep the roses her husband gives her for anniversaries. She found another way to preserve them this year. Mike presented her with a dozen roses for their fourth anniversary. After enjoying them in the vase for a few days, she removed the tops from the stems and arranged them bottom down in a crystal bowl with a few of the leaves for accent. They air dried in a week or so, and now they make a beautiful dried centerpiece. You may also add a tiny bit of rose potpourri oil every once in a while to remember the sweet fragrance of your special occasion.

But God made the earth by his power; he founded the world by his wisdom and stretched out the heavens by his understanding. When he thunders, the waters in the heavens roar; he makes clouds rise from the ends of the earth. He sends lightning with the rain and brings out the wind from his storehouses.

JEREMIAH 10:12

Captive Thoughts

> We demolish arguments and every pretension that sets itself up
> against the knowledge of God, and we take captive every thought
> to make it obedient to Christ.
>
> 2 CORINTHIANS 10:5

I've always been amazed at how quickly I can change my mind. This swing is usually dictated by new information or circumstances. Each thought prepares the way for the next. But if I'm not careful, before I know it, I can entertain thoughts that are anything but glorifying to God.

Paul instructs us to take every thought captive, meaning to hold them tight within boundaries or confines. One thing must be understood in order to live by this standard. The Enemy realizes that our minds are strongholds, either for him or for the Lord. We must recognize that we are incapable, on our own, of taking every thought captive. The spiritual warfare that has to be waged can only be won by the strength of God, not our weak human efforts. It is our act of complete surrender to His Spirit that allows Him to truly be Lord of our lives.

Ask the Lord to show you the heart behind your thoughts today. Allow Him to clean out those things that are standing in the way of your relationship with Him.

*T*he Arkansas amsonia is a showy perennial that changes drastically from spring to fall. Light blue star-shaped flowers and lovely green leaves grace this plant in the spring. In the fall, the flowers disappear, and the foliage becomes bright yellow.

Mike's Garden

When the woman saw that the fruit of the tree was good for food and
pleasing to the eye, and also desirable for gaining wisdom, she took
some and ate it. She also gave some to her husband, who was with her,
and he ate it. Then the eyes of both of them were opened, and they
realized they were naked; so they sewed fig leaves together and made
coverings for themselves. Then the man and his wife heard the sound of
the LORD God as he was walking in the garden in the cool of the day,
and they hid from the LORD God among the trees of the garden.
But the LORD God called to the man, "Where are you?"

GENESIS 3:6–9

Starla and her husband, Mike, have planted a vegetable garden for the last three years. Each year, their tomatoes and
peppers grow wonderfully, producing enough for all of us to have
plenty and give away baskets full. But each year, there has been
a problem with their sweet corn. Every spring, Mike would plant
the seeds exactly according to the seed company's directions. We
had plenty of rain and plenty of sunshine. But as the tomato
vines were stretching up and out and the pepper plants were
growing tall and leafy, only about half the corn had even
sprouted. The corn that did sprout was usually weak and hardly
ever produced even one disease-free ear. Soil testing showed deficiencies which could be corrected, but only if the soil was treated
each season.

When the Lord formed Adam from dirt, He created him in
His likeness, with no deficiencies. When Adam and Eve sinned,

they invited the first imperfections into their lives. Though they could still function well in many areas, they couldn't grow in their relationship with the Lord because they had become disobedient.

In the same way, our relationship with the Lord suffers when sin is present in our lives. When we are aware of being uncomfortable in His presence, it is a clear sign that the Holy Spirit is at work, treating our soil. He is faithful to will and to work in us for His good pleasure. His pleasure is derived from an honest relationship with us which produces a harvest of fruit in our lives, more beautiful than we have ever imagined.

My grandparents grew several varieties of iris in a corner of their vegetable garden. The irises in my garden are deep purple. Irises should be divided every three to four years for improvement and increase. Dividing should be done during the time of "rest," when their leaves are turning brown, a short time after they bloom.

God's Garden

It was he who gave some to be apostles, some to be prophets, some to be evangelists, and some to be pastors and teachers, to prepare God's people for works of service, so that the body of Christ may be built up until we all reach unity in the faith and in the knowledge of the Son of God and become mature, attaining to the whole measure of the fullness of Christ. Then we will no longer be infants, tossed back and forth by the waves, and blown here and there by every wind of teaching and by the cunning and craftiness of men in their deceitful scheming. Instead, speaking the truth in love, we will in all things grow up into him who is the Head, that is, Christ. From him the whole body, joined and held together by every supporting ligament, grows and builds itself up in love, as each part does its work.

EPHESIANS 4:11–16

In my garden, there are a variety of perennials. Some are large and have deep roots. Others were planted just this year. One variety called hostas provides a simple border under our windows, but also serves as the perfect backdrop for the blue hydrangeas' spectacular show in July and August. The hostas were here when we first moved into our home. At the time, I wasn't familiar with this stately plant. I simply loved the big green leaves. Imagine my surprise when I discovered another dimension to their personality appearing in the form of tiny white blossoms.

As I read this portion of Scripture, I noticed a striking similarity between a well-planned perennial garden and the body of Christ. Like the hostas, some members seem to have been around forever. They're very dependable, but at first glance, wouldn't appear to have much "flair." Then there are those who are like hyacinths, very fragrant and beautiful for a season, but needing other flowers to fill out the color and texture of the garden when they're dormant. To me, the variety in the garden is a lovely illustration of the body of Christ.

God has designed each member to serve a unique purpose in a particular season. Each one is beautiful individually, but it is only in the scheme of the entire garden that our true beauty is displayed to the world. Instead of competing for the most visible "container," or a place that would show off our glory, let us desire, in love for our Lord and for our brothers and sisters, to be seen as His garden, plantings of the Lord, that He may be glorified.

Some of the perennials in our ever-expanding garden include hostas, roses, and lilies. This coming year we have plans to add, among others, lily of the valley, several varieties of tulips, lots more lilies, and another hydrangea shrub. A new birdbath is planned for our feathered guests, and I'll probably add some wonderful blue Siberian irises.

How Beautiful

How beautiful the hands that served
The wine and the bread and the sons of the earth
How beautiful the feet that walked
The long dusty roads and the hill to the cross
How beautiful, how beautiful,
How beautiful is the Body of Christ
How beautiful the heart that bled
That took all my sin and bore it instead
How beautiful the tender eyes
That choose to forgive and never despise
How beautiful, how beautiful
How beautiful is the Body of Christ
And as He laid down His life
We offer this sacrifice
That we will live just as He died
Willing to pay the price
How beautiful the radiant bride
Who waits for her Groom with His light in her eyes
How beautiful when humble hearts give
The fruit of pure lives so that others may live
How beautiful, how beautiful
How beautiful is the Body of Christ
How beautiful the feet that bring
The sound of good news and the love of the King
How beautiful the hands that serve
The wine and the bread and the sons of the earth
How beautiful, how beautiful
How beautiful is the Body of Christ

Sitting in White

> *If we have been united with him like this in his death, we will*
> *certainly also be united with him in his resurrection.*
>
> ROMANS 6:5

My grandfather Paris was a minister. He was a gentle, unassuming man with a servant's heart and a tender love for God that never wavered. Grandma was the fiery, passionate one, but he was the rock at the center of our family. He also had a lovely tenor voice and was often asked to sing. Everyone's favorite was an old song about heaven called "Sitting in White" which depicts the eternal scene of worship at the throne of God. He usually finished the song with a catch in his voice and eyes bright with tears. The last time I heard him sing it was just a year before he died. At the end of the song he said, "Won't it be wonderful when we know we've finally made it?"

At the age of seventy-three, my grandpa suffered a massive heart attack and three days later went home to be with the Lord. I have two vivid memories of his funeral. One is a picture of my grandmother in a white linen dress. All her life she'd worn white to funerals "in honor of the Resurrection," and today would be no different. She had told me that after living with someone for forty-nine years you don't know how to live without him. And yet there she was—quietly declaring that her faith and hope were still in God.

When Grandpa had sung "Sitting in White" for the final time a year earlier, someone had had the wisdom to make a recording. At his funeral the tape was played, and as the song finished we all heard him say, "Won't it be wonderful when we know we've finally made it?"

My grandmother lived for fourteen more years. Though she never stopped missing her husband, she continued to be productive, joyful, and full of faith. And right up until her death, at the age of ninety-two, she still had that same fire. At her funeral, her five granddaughters were seated close together—all wearing white. Grandpa sang again and once more we heard him say, "Won't it be wonderful when we know we've finally made it?"

Sitting in White

Where anew the humble rainbow
Where extends the crystal sea
Dwells the redeemed, His glory to share
And they sang a new song saying,
"Holy blessed honor be unto the Lamb
Forever and e'er"

Sitting in white around the great throne
Having received the plaudit, "Well done"
Praising the Lamb whose blood has atoned
Sitting in white around the great throne

And the numbers of them were
Ten thousand times ten thousand and
Thousands and thousands from the earth gone
And the glorious multitude was
Countless as the seashore sand
Sitting in white around the great throne

Golden vials full of odor
Golden crowns of life they wore
Golden harps for everyone
And they rest not saying, "Holy, holy art thou Lord"
Sitting in white around the great throne

summer

Summer's garden bounty is usually met with an excitement for the harvest. Though the hours can be long and the heat oppressive, the gardener's great investment of labor motivates him to brave the elements to gather his garden's yield. He is delighted with the fruit of his labor, whether he is picking tomatoes at the peak of ripeness or cutting flowers for a colorful centerpiece. Sharing his abundance is the biggest thrill of all, as the gardener offers the benefits of all his hard work to those he loves.

The Lord is anxiously awaiting the day when He will gather us home. Yet there is still a big job to be done, and we all have a part in it. Matthew tells us that the harvest is plentiful, but the laborers are few. Jesus made the ultimate investment in the pursuit of His harvest. He invites us to follow His example and invest our lives in His vineyard, in order that His kingdom will be established in the hearts of men.

Good Fruits

But the fruit of the Spirit is love, joy, peace, patience, kindness, goodness, faithfulness, gentleness and self-control. Against such things there is no law. Those who belong to Christ Jesus have crucified the sinful nature with its passions and desires. Since we live by the Spirit, let us keep in step with the Spirit.

GALATIANS 5:22–25

*F*ruit is a very natural by-product of a tree or vine that is genuine, healthy, and planted in the right soil. The presence or absence of fruit in our lives becomes a test of whether or not we are truly living and walking in the Spirit of God. Although it is good to know what the fruits of the Spirit are and to work toward them as character goals, it is even more important to focus on an intimate relationship with Christ. When we truly belong to Him, and are full of His Spirit, the fruit will come in a very natural way. And it will be genuine.

*O*ne of my favorite summer pastimes is to take a drive down the country roads that are so abundant where we live. I try to drive slowly so that I'll be sure not to miss spotting any wild blackberry bushes that grow alongside the road. Blackberries are ripe for the picking when they drop into your hand with a gentle tug. They rarely make it to a jam or pie at our house — we like them straight from the bush!

Blue Is Becoming

> *Sing for joy in the LORD, O you righteous ones;*
>
> *praise is becoming to the upright.*
>
> PSALM 33:1 NASB

When I was a little girl, my grandmother told me that the color blue was becoming to me because I had blue eyes. She simply meant that I looked good in blue, and it's a funny thing—I still wear blue an awful lot!

So when I read in the Bible that "praise is becoming to the upright," I was struck by the thought that we as Christians are actually more beautiful when we worship. Of course this Scripture is referring to spiritual beauty, but I've noticed that it shines through. More than once I have looked around the room during worship and noticed faces that most people would consider plain looking positively radiant as they poured out their love and worship to their Father. And I've thought to myself, *If praise is this beautiful on the outside to my human eyes, how much more beautiful it must be on the inside to the eyes of a loving God.*

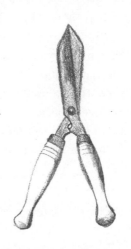

Blue hydrangeas are my favorite flowering shrub. They are enchanting in the garden, but their unique flowers also make lovely dried arrangements that provide a splash of color during cold winter months. Blue hydrangeas are blue due to the pH balance of the soil in which they are grown. There are products sold that change acid levels in soil, but here's an old-fashioned way to make white hydrangeas blue. Try adding your used morning coffee grounds to soil around the base of the shrub. When pruning most types of hydrangeas, make sure to do it <u>before</u> they set their buds. They usually set their buds for the next season right after they bloom.

Search My Heart

Search me, O God, and know my heart; test me and
know my anxious thoughts. See if there is any offensive
way in me, and lead me in the way everlasting.
PSALM 139:23–24

I had a friend in high school who knew me so well she could finish almost any sentence I started—and I could do the same for her. Because of this, we would often speak in a shorthand of interrupted sentences which made no sense at all to an outside listener, but which we understood completely. My friend knew me very, very well, but there were things even she couldn't know unless I chose to tell her.

God is the only one who literally knows each one of us better than we know ourselves. It's very significant that David asked God to search his heart. It was his heart. You would think he would be able to analyze it himself. But David understood something very important. We humans sometimes can be very wrong about the condition of our own hearts. We tend to be too hard on ourselves in some areas, and too easy in others. I believe the Enemy actually works at getting us to focus on small issues so that we continually overlook the critical ones—the big problems that often are the cause of most of the smaller ones. But when we ask the Spirit of God to search our hearts, His truth goes directly to the core like a laser. And if we allow it, He will remove all that should not be there and replace it with what should.

Search My Heart

Search my heart
Make me clean
It's your approval I long for
Rule my life
Be my King
Do what You will
I belong to You

*O*ne of our favorite hometown "lunch spots" is also a lovely bed-and-breakfast. Their acreage boasts over thirty magnolia trees, some of which were planted around the turn of the century. Magnolia trees may be trimmed in the middle of the summer when their leaves are full-sized, although it's best to plant them where they can grow and spread out fully without ever being trimmed.

Pressing On

> *Brothers, I do not consider myself yet to have taken hold of it.*
> *But one thing I do: Forgetting what is behind and straining*
> *toward what is ahead, I press on toward the goal to win the prize*
> *for which God has called me heavenward in Christ Jesus.*
>
> PHILIPPIANS 3:13–14

If you've attended a few of my concerts over the years, you know that I've always struggled with my weight. Around six years ago I reached a point where I was heavier than I had ever been. Because I just couldn't bear to document this trend, the frame of my album cover photos kept coming in tighter and tighter. By the time I recorded "Sanctuary," the cover revealed only part of my face. I commented wryly to a friend that if I continued to gain weight, the next album cover would simply be a picture of my nose.

Shortly thereafter, I felt the Lord was calling me to take a yearlong sabbatical for the purpose of spiritual, physical, and emotional rest and restoration. During that time at home, I was able to lose weight, and for the past five years I have maintained my weight within a normal range of a few pounds in either direction.

I learned and am still learning many things through this process, but one of the most important was the idea of pressing on. This is a concept I had put into practice in much of my life, but for some reason it had eluded me in an area where I needed it most. I had always had a tendency to be an all-or-nothing dieter. I would be very disciplined for a couple of weeks, then mess up and eat something against the rules. At that point, I had "failed." I would throw my hands in the air and eat everything in sight for the next three weeks. Of course, that system never worked.

Somehow this time was different. By the grace of God I was able to relax into a more effective approach. If I felt I had eaten the wrong thing, or even too much of the right thing, I began to simply say, "That was yesterday. Today we start again."

Not being perfect, I continued to have minor setbacks, but overall the new perspective kept me heading in the right direction. Finally the goal was reached and held. As I learned to press on in an area of weakness, I began to understand more than ever the value of this simple truth in every aspect of life.

We've all heard it said that a successful person is not one who has never failed but rather one who, when he does fail, always gets back up and keeps going. It occurred to me recently that when you are walking forward, if you fall flat on your face, just by getting up, you have gained a little ground. Of course this is a physical principle, but I believe there is truth in it that can be applied spiritually as well. I don't know any Christians who have never made a mistake. We all have. But the worst mistake is to allow failure or even fear of failure to paralyze you—to keep you lying flat on your face. The victorious Christian is the one who gets back up on his feet and, like Paul, forgets what is behind and presses on.

I'm not lookin' behind me
At mistakes I've already made
Hope is livin' inside me
I believe that my debts are paid
Trusting You now
I know I can make it
I made a vow
And I'm not gonna to break it
Lord, I'm keepin' my eyes on You
Following You, following You, my Lord

*T*here's nothing quite like the delicate scent of lilac drifting in your kitchen window to make you wish spring would go on forever. But because it only blooms for a very short time, you may want to dry lilac in order to preserve the gracious beauty of its flower throughout the year. To dry lilac, simply hang upside down in a cool dark room for five to ten days. You can also dry lilacs in silica gel (which can be found in craft stores) and use them alone or with other dried flowers to create simple and elegant wreaths and centerpieces.

Pretzels and Mustard

Again he said, "What shall we say the kingdom of God is like, or
what parable shall we use to describe it? It is like a mustard seed,
which is the smallest seed you plant in the ground. Yet when
planted, it grows and becomes the largest of all garden plants, with
such big branches that the birds of the air can perch in its shade."

MARK 4:30–32

One of my favorite snacks is pretzels and mustard (it can also be fat-free!). To think that such a potent and wonderful flavor can come something as tiny as a mustard seed is amazing. Yet the same can be said about the truth of God being planted in our lives.

When we allow what would seem to be the tiniest seed of truth to take root in our lives, the growth that results can be huge. It is also true, though, that in allowing destructive seeds like bitterness and unforgiveness to take root, we can expect a harvest that will have branches so large, they will shade and try to choke out every other planting of the Lord.

It is my experience that we can usually be counted on to be fertile ground. (Verse 27 of this chapter explains this.) The question that comes to my mind is, "Am I fertile to receive the crop that my Father has intended for me, or do I allow the seeds that the Father of Lies scatters to take root?" It is the Holy Spirit that alerts us to weeds from the Enemy, and it is the grace of the Lord that enables us to let those roots be pulled from our hearts.

*M*y favorite pretzel dip is just plain French's mustard. Starla likes to add a little honey for a different flavor. To try it her way, just mix four tablespoons of plain mustard with two and a half teaspoons of honey.

True Love

Dear friends, let us love one another, for love comes from God.
Everyone who loves has been born of God and knows God.
Whoever does not love does not know God, because God is love.
1 JOHN 4:7–8

ove is commonly thought of as an emotion—in many cases an uncomfortable emotion. But by commanding us to love one another God lets us know that He considers love to be a choice. He also makes it clear that true love is a very practical thing, and the evidence of love is not found only in what we say or even in what we feel. It will involve our hands, our time, our finances—literally our whole being—because real love is ultimately about what we do.

Seed sharing" programs are available in many gardening magazines and internet sites. These programs offer the opportunity to exchange seeds you have collected with those who have the exact item you've been searching for, but just can't seem to find in your "neck of the woods."

Feed the Birds

Then Jesus said to his disciples: "Therefore I tell you, do not worry about your life, what you will eat; or about your body, what you will wear. Life is more than food, and the body more than clothes. Consider the ravens: They do not sow or reap, they have no storeroom or barn; yet God feeds them. And how much more valuable you are than birds! Who of you by worrying can add a single hour to his life? Since you cannot do this very little thing, why do you worry about the rest? Consider how the lilies grow. They do not labor or spin. Yet I tell you, not even Solomon in all his splendor was dressed like one of these. If that is how God clothes the grass of the field, which is here today, and tomorrow is thrown into the fire, how much more will he clothe you, O you of little faith! And do not set your heart on what you will eat or drink; do not worry about it. For the pagan world runs after all such things, and your Father knows that you need them. But seek his kingdom, and these things will be given to you as well."

LUKE 12:22–31

We have bird feeders underneath the arbor in our backyard. Both Jack and I derive an amazing amount of pleasure from watching bluebirds, robins, hummingbirds, doves, and all the rest show up for brunch each morning. We even keep field glasses in a handy drawer in order to have a close-up view from time to time. My sisters have started calling me "the bird woman," and I'm not sure it's meant as a compliment, but it doesn't matter. I take too much delight in being able to play a small part in God's fulfillment of His promise to provide for even the birds of the air.

The birds don't understand the process of getting in the car, going to the store for seed, and remembering to fill up the feeders, but they have learned to be confident that there will always be food for them at our house. They don't worry about how it gets there.

God tells us to follow their example. If we begin to be anxious about earthly provision and worry about the future, it's a good sign that either we are not trusting God to keep His promise, or we have not been concerned with matters of His Kingdom and therefore have no right to claim His promise in the first place. Worries about life are always a warning to a believer that his priorities need to be realigned with the will of God.

Hummingbirds are delightful to watch. I always try to give them plenty of incentive to be frequent visitors. Honeysuckle, petunias, and salvia are some of their favorite nectar stops. They also enjoy dropping by for a quick refresher at our hummingbird feeders. We use a recipe that is one part sugar to four parts water, boiled and cooled. (Be sure to clean the feeders every 4–5 days so the nectar won't ferment.)

A friend of ours, who is a master gardener, gets hummingbirds to sit on her fingers and drink. She brings her hummingbird feeder in her house at noon, then carries it back to the same location at 4:00 P.M. She holds the feeder perfectly still, and the hummingbirds come sit on her fingers and drink.

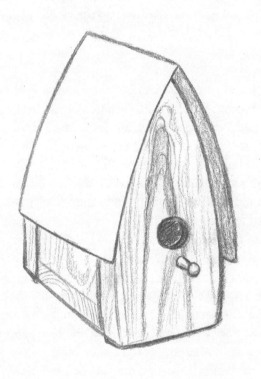

Ten-Mile Hike

Watch the path of your feet, and all your ways will be established.
Do not turn to the right nor to the left; turn your foot from evil.

PROVERBS 4:26–27 NASB

We have some wonderful nature trails in northwest Arkansas. Angie and I especially love discovering and hiking new paths through the woods. Early one Saturday morning we set off on what we thought was an easy, three-mile hike. We planned to have breakfast afterward.

On this particular trail, the path is marked intermittently by a splash of blue paint on various tree trunks. It's a subtle system and possible to miss, but if you're paying attention, the signs appear just often enough to keep you headed in the right direction. Angie and I were having a great time talking and walking (sometimes climbing), admiring wildflowers and butterflies, when somehow we took a wrong turn. Initially, though it was the wrong one, we still appeared to be on a clear trail. So we didn't even notice that we hadn't seen any blue paint for a very long time. Only when the path became increasingly rough and steep did we begin to question our navigation. However, by that time we had gone so far that we couldn't imagine turning around. We kept pushing on—sure that this trail would eventually lead "somewhere." Besides, there was evidence that others had been there before us—a soft drink can, a candy wrapper—"so it must be a good trail." (Later, we began to realize they'd probably "been there" on four-wheelers—not on foot!)

After more than two hours, having come before breakfast and without provisions, we were very thirsty, very hungry, and a little scared. I was afraid we might have wandered into mountain lion territory and I knew, positively, we were in copperhead territory. Finally, we arrived at a clearing on top of a mountain. From that vantage point we were able to see that we were absolutely in the dead center of nowhere!

With heavy hearts, we made the decision to turn around—carefully retracing our steps until we saw, with great relief, a tree with blue paint on the trunk. Now it was easy to see where we'd made our mistake, and we continued on from where we'd left off. We both quickly noticed that our steps were lighter, we were no longer afraid, and even the hunger and thirst didn't seem so bad. We still had no clue where we were, but we knew we were going the right way because we were following the signs left by someone who had been there before us.

As we walked, our conversation turned to the fact that this experience was very similar to something that also occurs in our spiritual lives. God speaks to us clearly, but quietly. If we allow ourselves to be distracted, we can quickly wander very far from His chosen path—without even knowing it. When we realize our error, it can be a great temptation to continue on our own path—simply because we have made such an investment of time and energy there. But if we do, we remain subject to the fear and exhaustion that always accompany those who know in their hearts that they are traveling a road to nowhere.

The only way back is to turn decisively away from the wrong path and begin to listen closely, once more, for His still, small voice. When we know we are following Him, that is all we need to know. There is no reason to fear, and we find again the joy, confidence, and enthusiasm that come from the simple knowledge that we are going in the right direction.

For a relaxing bath, add fifteen drops of lavender oil to warm bath water. Soak for twenty minutes, allowing the oils to moisturize and soften your skin. After bathing, pat dry with a thick towel scented beforehand with your favorite body spray. (It's nice to use a warm towel straight from the dryer.) I've found that a warm and pleasantly scented bath always helps to soothe tired muscles, calm my spirit, and quiet my mind after a busy day or a stressful weekend.

Where He Leads Me

There is a great, broad road through the meadow
And many travel there
But I have a gentle shepherd I would follow anywhere
Up a narrow path, through the mountains
To the valley far below
To be ever in His presence, where He leads me I will go
Where He leads me I will go

There are many wondrous voices
Day and night, they fill the air
But there is one so small and quiet
I would know it anywhere
In the city or in the wilderness, there's a ringing, crystal clear
To be ever close beside Him, when He calls me I will hear
When He calls me I will hear

Where He leads me, I will follow
When He calls me, I will hear
Where He leads me, I will follow
When He calls me, I will hear

There is a great, broad road to nowhere
And so many travel there
But I have a gentle shepherd I would follow anywhere
Though the journey take me far away
From the place I call my home
To be ever in His presence, where He leads me I will go
Where He leads me I will go

"Where He Leads Me" originally recorded on "My Utmost for His Highest" (Myrrh/Word Records) © 1993 Ariose Music/Mountain Spring Music (Adm. by EMI Christian Music Publishing)—ASCAP.

Simple Truth

O LORD, our Lord, how majestic is your name in all the earth! You have
set your glory above the heavens. From the lips of children and infants
you have ordained praise because of your enemies, to silence the foe and
the avenger. When I consider your heavens, the work of your fingers, the
moon and the stars, which you have set in place, what is man that you
are mindful of him, the son of man that you care for him? You made him
a little lower than the heavenly beings and crowned him with glory and
honor. You made him ruler over the works of your hands; you put everything under his feet: all flocks and herds, and the beasts of the field, the
birds of the air, and the fish of the sea, all that swim the paths of the seas.
O LORD, our Lord, how majestic is your name in all the earth!

PSALM 8

An old friend of mine named Neil was four years old when I
heard him pray this prayer aloud. "Thank You, God,
because if it wasn't for You, it wouldn't be for us." The grammar
is charming, but the message is powerful. God has often brought
this prayer to my memory when I needed to be reminded of its
simple truth.

How easy it is for us to forget where we came from, who we are
without God, and who He is. When my heart is in the right
place I will be filled with wonder and humility that the Creator
of the universe has chosen to lift me up, to care for me, and to
receive my praise. So today I remind myself once again that He
owes me nothing. He has given me everything, and it is my
incredible privilege simply to be called to worship Him.

What Am I Without You

You are the love of all my life
You are the living spring
You are the joy that finds my heart
Giver of all good things

What am I without You
What am I without You

You are the day that rules the night
You are the hope in me
All that I have descends from You
All I could ever be

What am I without You
What am I without You

What am I but a piece of earth
Breathing holy breath
What am I but a wayward child
Given life for certain death

You are the everlasting Lord
You are the risen King
That You would come and fill my soul
This is beyond a dream

What am I without You
What am I without You

"What Am I Without You" originally recorded on "Beyond a Dream" (Star Song Records) © 1993 Ariose Music/Mountain Spring Music—ASCAP.

God's Faithfulness

The LORD reigns forever; he has established his throne for judgment. He will judge the world in righteousness; he will govern the peoples with justice. The LORD is a refuge for the oppressed, a stronghold in times of trouble. Those who know your name will trust in you, for you, LORD, have never forsaken those who seek you.

PSALM 9:7–10

We trust in God because of His faithfulness. The more we know Him, the easier it is to trust Him, because we have seen over and over, up close, that His words are true and He does not forsake those who seek Him. Most of us have at least one friend that we know so well we would assume the best about her even if circumstances indicated otherwise. This is the level of relationship we should have with God, and it can only happen by spending time with Him. If we know God intimately, then our faith in Him will never be based on our circumstances—but always in His unchanging character.

When arranging cut flowers, always make their final cuts underwater and fill the vase with warm water. This decreases the chance for air bubbles to form in the freshly cut stems, which would prevent their water intake and shorten their vase life.

You Have Been Good

Oh Lord, You have been good
You have been faithful to all generations
Oh Lord, Your steadfast love
And tender mercy has been our salvation
For by Your hand we have been fed
And by Your Spirit we have been led
Oh Lord, You have been good
You have been faithful, You have been good

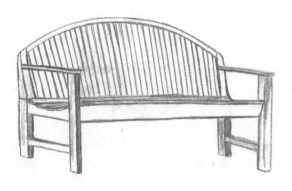

Share the Harvest

The word of the LORD came to me, saying, "Before I formed you in
the womb I knew you, before you were born I set you apart; I
appointed you as a prophet to the nations." "Ah, Sovereign LORD,"
I said, "I do not know how to speak; I am only a child." But the
LORD said to me, "Do not say, 'I am only a child.' You must go to
everyone I send you to and say whatever I command you. Do not
be afraid of them, for I am with you and will rescue you," declares
the LORD. Then the LORD reached out his hand and touched my
mouth and said to me, "Now, I have put my words in your mouth.
See, today I appoint you over nations and kingdoms to uproot and
tear down, to destroy and overthrow, to build and to plant."

JEREMIAH 1:4–10

This was the word of the Lord to the prophet Jeremiah, and I believe it is also the word of the Lord to His children today. We should never say, "I'm too young" or "I'm too shy; I don't have the right gifts or talents." If you say those things, you set limits on God's plan for your life. God says, "I have put My words in your mouth." That means you can do and say things that go far beyond your own personality or abilities, and there is no need to be afraid. God is sending a new generation out in His name with authority to speak His words to the nations. Each of us must answer this one question: "Will I be obedient to His call on my life?"

Faithful Men

Come and join the reapers
All the kingdom seekers
Laying down your life to find it in the end
Come and share the harvest
Help to light the darkness
For the Lord is calling faithful men

"Faithful Men" originally recorded on "Kingdom Seekers" (Star Song Records) ©
1985 StraightWay Music/Mountain Spring Music—ASCAP.

$\mathcal{A}$s the rain

and the snow come down from

heaven, and do not return to it without

watering the earth and making it bud and

flourish, so that it yields seed for the sower

and bread for the eater, so is my word that

goes out from my mouth: It will not return

to me empty, but will accomplish what

I desire and achieve the purpose

for which I sent it.

ISAIAH 55:10

Be Careful

So, if you think you are standing firm, be careful that you don't
fall! No temptation has seized you except what is common to
man. And God is faithful; he will not let you be tempted beyond
what you can bear. But when you are tempted, he will also pro-
vide a way out so that you can stand up under it.

1 CORINTHIANS 10:12–13

Complacency when things are going well may be one of the
most common mistakes made by Christians. We are only able
to stand by the grace of God. If we try to make it on our own, it
is only a matter of time until we fall. But the good news is, if we
remember that God is our strength, we can withstand any temptation. As long as we are truly depending on God, He will not let
us fall. That is His promise, and He is faithful.

Father, please keep us from the sin of trusting in our own flesh.

Black tea is often included in organic sunburn treat-
ments. Oatmeal and cucumbers are also used in these
preparations to promote healing and bring relief to the skin.

The Highest Calling

Your attitude should be the same as that of Christ Jesus: Who,
being in very nature God, did not consider equality with God
something to be grasped, but made himself nothing, taking the very
nature of a servant, being made in human likeness. And being
found in appearance as a man, he humbled himself and became
obedient to death—even death on a cross! Therefore God exalted
him to the highest place and gave him the name that is above every
name, that at the name of Jesus every knee should bow, in heaven
and on earth and under the earth, and every tongue confess that
Jesus Christ is Lord, to the glory of God the Father.

PHILIPPIANS 2:5–11

At Youth With A Mission in Arkansas, we have a ministry-wide picnic every September—usually at one of the nearby lakes. Everyone spends the day swimming, boating, hiking, and taking part in all sorts of organized games and activities, including eating! Everyone, that is, except the ministry leaders. They spend the day grilling hamburgers and hot dogs for almost three hundred people, cleaning up after them, and doing all the other necessary tasks. They spend the day literally serving those they lead, an attitude of the heart which is evident in their lives year-round.

So often we tend to look down on positions of service—setting our sights, instead, on higher positions that appear to bring with them privilege, authority, and respect. What we forget is that Jesus Himself chose to be a servant, and the greatest privilege we can have is that of following His example. To lay down our rights, our ambitions, and our lives in obedience to the Father is actually the highest calling in the Kingdom of God.

Keeper of the Door

I dreamed I saw my name in lights
And spoke Your Word for all to hear
I dreamed my name was recognized by people far
    and people near
But I have come to understand like David long ago
That humble service in Your house
Is still the greatest dream a heart can hold

Oh let me be a servant
A keeper of the door
My heart is only longing
To see forevermore
The glory of Your presence
The dwelling of the Lord
Oh let me be a servant
A keeper of the door

The one who was no less than God
Took on the flesh of lowly man
And came to wash the feet of clay
Because it was Your holy plan
And I, no greater than my King, would ever seek a place
Of humble service in Your house
To gaze into the light that is Your face

Oh let me be a servant
A keeper of the door
My heart is only longing
To see forevermore
The glory of Your presence
The dwelling of the Lord
Oh let me be a servant
A keeper of the door

Here's a tried-and-true way to peel ripe roma tomatoes before cooking or freezing. Bring 6 cups of water to a boil and prepare a deep bowl with 4 cups ice-cold water. Dip the whole tomatoes in the boiling water for about 10 seconds, then in the ice water for another 10 seconds. Trim the tops off and squeeze the bottom. The tomato should easily slip right out of the skin. Puree in a blender or food processor. Slowly simmer and reduce 2–3 hours or until juice thickens. Now it's ready to be included in your favorite pasta sauce!

Garden Fresh Marinara

6 cups roma tomato puree
1/2 cup finely chopped onions (optional)
1/2 cup finely chopped green peppers (optional)
1/2 cup virgin olive oil
1 tbsp. sugar
1 tsp. basil
1/4 tsp. salt
1 tsp. oregano
3 medium cloves fresh garlic, finely minced
2 tsp. cayenne
pinch of paprika
Freshly grated parmesan cheese

In large saucepan, slowly sauté onions and green peppers in 2 tbsp. olive oil. Cook until onions are translucent and peppers are soft. Add minced garlic and continue to sauté for 1 minute, stirring constantly. Add tomato puree, all spices and sugar, and remaining olive oil. Simmer for 30 minutes. Serve over cooked pasta (my favorite is angel hair). Garnish with freshly grated parmesan cheese. Makes four "pasta bowl" size servings. This dish is also great topped with grilled chicken breast.

Storms

One day Jesus said to his disciples, "Let's go over to the other side of the lake." So they got into a boat and set out. As they sailed, he fell asleep. A squall came down on the lake, so that the boat was being swamped, and they were in great danger. The disciples went and woke him, saying, "Master, Master, we're going to drown!" He got up and rebuked the wind and the raging waters; the storm subsided, and all was calm. "Where is your faith?" he asked his disciples. In fear and amazement they asked one another, "Who is this? He commands even the winds and the water, and they obey him."

LUKE 8:22–25

At certain times of the year, tornadoes are common in Arkansas. One evening when I was ten years old, we were driving home from a trip out of town. As we got closer to Springdale, we heard on the car radio that a tornado had touched down, and we began to see the evidence that a storm had truly been in the area.

When we reached town, we had to search for an alternate route home because so many streets were blocked. As we drove through the devastation, picking our way around debris, there was a growing sense of awareness that when we finally did reach our house, it might not be there. Looking back as an adult, I have an even greater appreciation for my parents' conversation in the car that night. They quickly focused themselves and their children on the underlying fact that God is faithful. Whether or not we still had a house was ultimately not the point. God had always taken care of us, and He always would.

Our house was there and, unlike many of the homes close by, was undamaged. But I will never forget the lesson I learned that night. It is our response to the storms in life that determines the amount of power they will have over us.

Some of the most frightening storms can actually be inside your own heart. On the outside everything can appear completely calm—so that even your best friends don't realize you're filled with raging anxiety, fear, and dread. But Jesus knows exactly how you feel and even why, and He gently asks, "Where is your faith?" His voice can calm the storm in your heart just as surely as it did the winds and water in the passage above. Take a moment from the assault of the day, listen to the quiet words of authority in your spirit, and obey.

Peace Be Still

There is an ocean inside my heart
Mostly the water is calm
Just enough breeze to keep me sailing
I feel safe and warm
Angry winds blow suddenly
How this world can threaten me
Then the Master speaks with sure authority

Peace be still, Peace be still
Peace be still to the wind and the waves
Peace be still, Peace be still
Peace be still and the ocean obeys

There is an ocean inside my heart
Mostly the water is calm
Just enough breeze to keep me sailing
I feel safe and warm
Angry winds blow suddenly
I become a churning sea
Then I hear a quiet voice — He says to me

Peace be still, Peace be still
Peace be still to the wind and the waves
Peace be still, Peace be still
Peace be still and the ocean obeys

"Peace Be Still" originally recorded on "For Every Heart"
(Star Song Records) © 1988 Ariose Music/Mountain Spring
Music—ASCAP.

Moonflowers are an incredibly fragrant evening bloomer. These pure white annuals with slight green tinges open gently every night as the sun sets, and close again at morning's first light. A cricket's song and the sweet perfume of moonflowers are the perfect pairing for an otherwise still summer night.

Gethsemane

> *Then Jesus went with his disciples to a place called Gethsemane,*
> *and he said to them, "Sit here while I go over there and pray." He*
> *took Peter and the two sons of Zebedee along with him, and he*
> *began to be sorrowful and troubled. Then he said to them, "My soul*
> *is overwhelmed with sorrow to the point of death. Stay here and*
> *keep watch with me." Going a little farther, he fell with his face to*
> *the ground and prayed, "My Father, if it is possible, may this cup be*
> *taken from me. Yet not as I will, but as you will."*
>
> MATTHEW 26:36–39

Last summer my brother Oren and I traveled to Israel, where we had the opportunity to visit Gethsemane. Moved by the peaceful quiet of the ancient grove of olive trees, we were reminded that when Jesus needed to be alone with His Father and reveal the deepest concerns of His heart, He went to a garden to pray.

I find that many times, when I need solace, I also retreat to the garden to talk with the Lord. In all our lives there are moments when we know that only our Heavenly Father will truly understand what we're going through. There is something about being surrounded by the beauty and quiet of His creation that inspires our lips and our spirits to worship Him—and reminds our hearts that He is the Lord . . . He is God.

*O*live oils are graded according to their acidity. There are three main grades of olive oil: extra virgin, virgin, and pure. Extra virgin olive oil is only one percent acid. Virgin olive oil has a slightly higher acidity level, which ranges from one to three percent. Extra virgin and virgin olive oils are the result of "cold-pressing." Pure olive oil is considered a commercial grade, and is the result of a second pressing using heat.

Grandmother's Sunbonnet

Therefore put on the full armor of God, so that when the day of evil comes, you may be able to stand your ground, and after you have done everything, to stand. Stand firm then, with the belt of truth buckled around your waist, with the breastplate of right-eousness in place, and with your feet fitted with the readiness that comes from the gospel of peace. In addition to all this, take up the shield of faith, with which you can extinguish all the flaming arrows of the evil one. Take the helmet of salvation and the sword of the Spirit, which is the word of God.

EPHESIANS 6:13–17

As children, we often watched my Grandma Paris in her garden, her face hidden by the brim of her bonnet, working to keep the weeds out and the vegetables in. Wearing her bonnet was a necessity, as she saw it, for gardening. As we grew older, she made bonnets for my sisters and me and then let us "help" her pick as many green beans, tomatoes, and okra as we could. She became a beautiful example of more than one important principle as we watched her get her skilled hands dirty. While she worked, her bonnet covered her face so that anyone passing by would have simply seen her as a gardener, not Mary Lydia Paris. In the same way, as I make the choice to be conformed to the Lord's image and covered by Him, people passing by will see Christ, instead of me.

Another benefit my grandma's bonnet provided was protection from the harmful rays of the sun. As I allow the Lord to cultivate and change my life, I can expect criticism from an ungodly world. It is God's grace, however, that protects me. Our bonnets were made of cheerful gingham and were usually trimmed in lace with sashes to tie under our chins. Ephesians 6 describes a different sort of protection no less beautiful to the child of God. His "Father heart" is clearly demonstrated as He shields us from the world, and lets us "help" Him in *His* garden.

There is a perennial named "Granny's Bonnet" that responds well to either full sun or partial shade. The blossoms come out in the middle of summer in a variety of beautiful hues — red, purple, white, and pink — and grow wonderfully in sunny borders.

autumn

*A*utumn is characterized by a crispness in the air and the unmistakable scent of fallen leaves. It is also a time for pruning and setting out new bulbs. Tulips, hyacinths, and lilies are put to bed, looking forward to their debut in the coming spring. A wise gardener will plant them at a depth that will protect them from predators, and place mulch at first freeze to defend them from the harsh temperatures and winds of winter. Silver spruce trees, among others, require an autumn pruning in order to grow their best in the following seasons.

This garden activity reminds me of our Heavenly Father's attentiveness as He plants and prunes in our lives. John 15:2 explains that we are pruned in order that we may produce even more fruit. Each time the Lord prunes us, He is always watching over us, trimming from our lives the things that keep us from being all He has designed us to be. He chooses the perfect time for our pruning, even though sometimes it doesn't feel like the best time to us.

Clean House

> *I will sing of your love and justice; to you, O LORD, I will sing praise. I will be careful to lead a blameless life—when will you come to me? I will walk in my house with blameless heart. I will set before my eyes no vile thing.*
>
> PSALM 101:1–3

I remember singing this song in Sunday school, and you probably do too.

> *Be careful little eyes what you see*
> *Be careful little eyes what you see*
> *For the Father up above is looking down in love*
> *So be careful little eyes what you see*

As Christians, we know that our body is the temple of the Holy Spirit. But we often forget that what our eyes see affects our spirit, and therefore the dwelling place of God. If we would use our spiritual eyes to truly see our body as the "home" of the Lord, we would probably be much more careful about the trash we bring in and scatter around. Every command the Lord gives is for our good; every principle is grounded in love.

Matthew 6:22 tells us, "The eye is the lamp of the body. If your eyes are good, your whole body will be full of light. But if your eyes are bad, your whole body will be full of darkness. If then the light within you is darkness, how great is that darkness!" Would we come into God's house and turn out lights? That is exactly what we do when we place things before our eyes that are against the commands of the Lord. We must keep our sight pure before the Lord in order to keep His house clean and our lives in order.

It's a good idea to clean previously used planting pots before reusing. Just immerse the pots in a mixture of bleach and water for a few seconds, rinse well, and then let them air dry. This helps to ensure that any leftover bacteria will be removed, making new residents feel much more at home.

Be Holy

Therefore, prepare your minds for action; be self-controlled; set
your hope fully on the grace to be given you when Jesus Christ is
revealed. As obedient children, do not conform to the evil desires
you had when you lived in ignorance. But just as he who called you
is holy, so be holy in all you do; for it is written: "Be holy, because I
am holy." Since you call on a Father who judges each man's work
impartially, live your lives as strangers here in reverent fear. For
you know that it was not with perishable things such as silver or gold
that you were redeemed from the empty way of life handed down to
you from your forefathers, but with the precious blood of Christ, a
lamb without blemish or defect. He was chosen before the creation
of the world, but was revealed in these last times for your sake.
Through him you believe in God, who raised him from the dead and
glorified him, and so your faith and hope are in God.

1 PETER 1:13–21

I believe we sometimes take too lightly God's command to be
holy. We think, "Surely He didn't mean for us to be holy in
all we do—that just wouldn't be possible." Well, like so many of
His instructions, this one wouldn't be possible if we had to do it
on our own. If we will make the choice to obey, God will provide
the ability—just as He provided the sacrifice that redeemed us.

If you're having trouble even making the choice, if true holiness seems like too hard a thing and you've been tempted to give
up the fight and simply let your flesh rule because it's easier, take

a few moments today to consider again the high cost of your redemption. The precious blood of Jesus Christ was not easily spilled. We are not called to take the easy road but to follow the loving example of Christ. When we have really seen Him, obedience is the only choice.

Planting tomato roots six inches deep keeps their roots cooler and allows them to continue producing fruit when temperatures soar into the nineties. Morning watering also aids in keeping roots cool and productive during the warmest summer months.

Wise Investment

A generous man will himself be blessed, for he
shares his food with the poor.

PROVERBS 22:9

My husband, Jack, is generous almost to a fault—if that's possible. He's been known to pick up hitchhikers and buy them a hotel room for the night. (Not any more now that he's married!) The point is he feels the needs of others as if they were his own. If it's in his power he wants to do something about it. He's not foolish or gullible, but he does have the gift of mercy.

As a wife, I would so much rather be married to a generous man than a greedy one, even though it may mean we have less money in the bank. The result is we have more treasure in heaven. God promises that those who share with others will in turn be blessed by Him. Generosity in the name of the Lord, to those in need, is the wisest kind of investment.

When purchasing bulbs for fall planting, be sure they are firm and heavy. Soft bulbs could indicate rot. Planting bulbs good and deep (follow package directions for different varieties) helps to discourage squirrels and gophers from breaking the eighth commandment (Exodus 20:15)!

His Rules

There is a way that seems right to a man,
but in the end it leads to death.

PROVERBS 14:12

I think this verse has never been illustrated so widely as it is in our society today. Long ago, the Judge of the earth gave us laws and principles by which to govern our lives. His motives were love and justice, and His rules represented perfect wisdom. Through the ages humankind has proven over and over that obedience brings life and disobedience brings death. And yet now more than ever, deceived men and women stand in defiance of God. They say His laws are not valid. His principles no longer apply in this enlightened society. They believe they have changed the rules; moved the boundaries. But in reality the lines of good and evil have never moved an inch since they were first drawn by the hand of God. Millions of blinded souls step over the lines every day. It seems right to them, but they are walking purposely toward their own death. As children of God, we have an awesome responsibility to hold up the truth for others and to keep our eyes fixed on Jesus so that our hearts and minds will always be protected from the subtle deceptions of the age.

God is in control
We believe that His children
    will not be forsaken
God is in control
We will choose to remember
    and never be shaken
There is no power above or
    beside Him we know
Oh, God is in control

Matthew 18

If your brother sins against you, go and show him
his fault, just between the two of you. If he listens
to you, you have won your brother over.

MATTHEW 18:15

Years ago, Dad felt the Lord leading him to teach the principles of Matthew 18 in a way that could be easily understood and applied in everyday life.

There are always a lot of young people at Youth With A Mission, which is our home fellowship. Initially, a few in the group got very excited about Dad's teaching and began looking for every opportunity to confront anyone for the slightest perceived offense. Others, more frightened of confrontation, were tempted to ignore the teaching altogether. Of course, there is an appropriate balance between these two responses.

The time to go to a brother about a fault is when it continues to interfere with your relationship and you find yourself wanting to talk about him to others. Then the Word of God says you must confront him. In my experience, if you approach the one who has offended you in a spirit of humility, most often he will accept your correction and you will have gained him as a brother.

For most of us, this can be a difficult principle to follow, especially at first. But if we would all be very firm with ourselves in this area, I'm convinced there would be much greater unity in the body of Christ. Is there something between you and a brother or sister? I encourage you to go today and win them back—for the sake of Christ.

It's best to remove flower heads when they begin to fade. This allows all the plant's energy to be diverted to the roots.

Run, Starla, Run

And you have forgotten that word of encouragement that addresses you as sons: "My son, do not make light of the Lord's discipline, and do not lose heart when he rebukes you, because the Lord disciplines those he loves, and he punishes everyone he accepts as a son." Endure hardship as discipline; God is treating you as sons. For what son is not disciplined by his father? If you are not disciplined (and everyone undergoes discipline), then you are illegitimate children and not true sons. Moreover, we have all had human fathers who disciplined us and we respected them for it. How much more should we submit to the Father of our spirits and live! Our fathers disciplined us for a little while as they thought best; but God disciplines us for our good, that we may share in his holiness. No discipline seems pleasant at the time, but painful. Later on, however, it produces a harvest of righteousness and peace for those who have been trained by it. Therefore, strengthen your feeble arms and weak knees. "Make level paths for your feet," so that the lame may not be disabled, but rather healed.

HEBREWS 12:5–13

*O*nce, when Starla was very young, she successfully evaded our grandmother's attempts to spank her for almost a solid hour, with a complex series of maneuvers involving alternately hiding and running. Grandma finally stopped and called to my sister, who was partially hidden by a rosebush at the other end of the garden, "That's fine. Eventually, you'll have to come back to the house. And when you do, I'm gonna wear you out."

Of course, she loved her granddaughter very dearly—loved her enough to do whatever it took to make sure the seeds of righteousness were planted in her young heart.

When we receive discipline from the Lord, the human impulse is to struggle and resist. Of course, this is never a good idea, not with Grandma—and not with God. In the first place, running is pointless, and more importantly, it shows that we do not fully appreciate the incredible privilege of being called sons and daughters of God. Every time His discipline comes into our lives, it does His good work in our hearts and proves once more His great love for us.

Purple coneflowers are one of our favorite perennials. In addition to their longevity and hardiness, we all love the fact that butterflies are crazy about them.

Obedience Is Better

> But Samuel replied: "Does the LORD delight in burnt offerings and sacrifices as much as in obeying the voice of the LORD? To obey is better than sacrifice, and to heed is better than the fat of the rams."
>
> 1 SAMUEL 15:22

I learned the lesson of this passage as a very little girl. One day when I had been bad, I hit upon a brilliant plan. Little did I know it was the same plan used for thousands of years by children everywhere—including my mother. I rushed out to the garden to pick a bouquet of roses, knowing she would be so overcome with gratitude and delight that she would not be able to find it in her heart to punish me for my crime. With a little luck, she might even be so distracted that she would forget about it altogether.

Of course, you're already way ahead of me, because you tried to do this too. You know that my mom graciously thanked me for my gift, then sat down and took the time to teach me that obedience was much more important than sacrifice, not only to her, but to God.

We all know that God wants our obedience, not our sacrifices, but sometimes the Enemy can still tempt us to try to bribe God with our adult versions of a bouquet from the garden. The next time you offer a sacrifice to the Lord, take a moment to check your heart and make sure it's a sacrifice of love, not a substitute for obedience.

*O*ur lives are pleasing to the Lord when we learn the lesson exemplified by the Obedient plant. The flowers of this lovely perennial can be turned in any direction on the stem, and they remain in that position without turning back.

Wounds from a Friend

Wounds from a friend can be trusted,
but an enemy multiplies kisses.
PROVERBS 27:6

Most of us struggle with a tendency to be defensive when someone shares with us an area of weakness in our lives. Yet we should be grateful for brothers and sisters who love us so much that they're willing to risk their relationship with us in order to speak the truth. It's easy to be the one who's always popular—the one who always tells us what we want to hear. But our truest friends are those who tell us what we need to hear. It may hurt at first, but in the end, truth ministers life. We may not have many friends who are this committed to us. The ones we have are treasures and should never be taken for granted.

Thank You, Lord, for my true friends.

Seems like you know when I need you
Seems like He knows who to send
You never come as a prophet
Just an open-hearted friend
Faithfully wounding my pride
Bringing me back to His side
Sharing the Word that you hide in your heart
You are a true friend
Pointing me to Him
Lifting my downcast eyes
Turning my wandering gaze to the sky
Proving your love again
You are a true friend

It's Not My Job

> "Do not judge, or you too will be judged. For in the same way
> you judge others, you will be judged, and with the measure you
> use, it will be measured to you. Why do you look at the speck of
> sawdust in your brother's eye and pay no attention to the plank
> in your own eye? How can you say to your brother, 'Let me take
> the speck out of your eye,' when all the time there is a plank in
> your own eye? You hypocrite, first take the plank out of your
> own eye, and then you will see clearly to remove the speck from
> your brother's eye."
>
> MATTHEW 7:1–5

It can be a great temptation to look around and try to analyze
the actions and motives of our brothers and sisters. Of course
we can only guess at someone else's motivation, so our judgments
are often very wrong—which is one reason Jesus told us not to
judge. It simply is not our responsibility. Judging others also
becomes a convenient distraction from analyzing our own
actions and motives—which is our responsibility. When my
heart is in the right place I'm actually very glad it's not my job
to evaluate those around me. It's an awesome thing to pronounce
judgment, and only God has the wisdom and authority to do it.

*Father, please give me the grace to be concerned with the motiva-
tions of my own heart, and to remember that You alone are the judge
of the earth.*

*T*he other day I walked out my door and smelled the sweetest perfume in the air. I followed the scent to a single hyacinth bloom. The Bible tells us in 2 Corinthians 2:14–17 that our lives should possess a godly fragrance that literally draws people to find the Source.

Marcel's Orchard

> *"Even now the reaper draws his wages, even now he harvests the crop for eternal life, so that the sower and the reaper may be glad together. Thus the saying 'One sows and another reaps' is true. I sent you to reap what you have not worked for. Others have done the hard work, and you have reaped the benefits of their labor."*
>
> JOHN 4:36–38

In the early days of Youth With A Mission, Arkansas, a young farmer from Vermont, named Marcel Lebeau, came with his wife and two young sons to receive training and begin work in full-time ministry. The staff and students at YWAM have always been a close-knit, Christian community, some of them living on the actual campus, and many more nearby in the surrounding neighborhood.

Marcel and his family settled easily into the fellowship. While he and his wife, Fran, attended the Discipleship Training School and the School of Evangelism, their two boys were enrolled in the private Christian school located on the campus. When their training was completed, both Marcel and Fran found great joy in beginning to fill the place in God's kingdom to which they knew He had called them. Marcel had a true heart for sharing the love of Christ with others, not only during "Missionary Outreaches" in foreign countries, but also with those much closer to home. Wherever he went, his gracious demeanor gently opened hearts to hear his message. His identification with the heart of God eventually extended to a deep concern for unwed mothers and their children. He had a dream to see a local crisis pregnancy center and home for unwed mothers established, and he worked diligently and tirelessly to help motivate others to be involved.

Marcel always looked for opportunities to serve those around him in practical ways. One day he asked for permission to plant an apple orchard on top of a hill in the center of the campus. It would beautify the property and someday produce fruit for those who lived and worked there. He lovingly and faithfully tended the young seedlings as a simple offering to the Lord. I often noticed him working quietly, after hours, in the orchard and tried to imagine the full-grown apple trees that I somehow knew he could see clearly.

Marcel never actually saw his trees bear fruit. When the orchard was still very young, he was diagnosed with a very aggressive form of cancer. Barely six months later, he was gone. We were relieved that his pain was over and we rejoiced that he was with Jesus, whom he loved so much. And yet we all grieved, along with his family, for this quiet, tenderhearted man who understood so well the value of planting seeds.

That was thirteen years ago. Just the other day Starla called me and said, "The apples are on and they're delicious! We need to make a pie." I agreed. I hadn't thought of Marcel in a while—but now I did. I thought about the mature orchard bearing beautiful and abundant fruit which blessed an entire community—including me. I thought about Marcel's dream, fulfilled after his death: a crisis pregnancy center and a home for unwed mothers, built and staffed by the united efforts of the body of Christ in our area. I thought about the babies whose lives had been saved; the young mothers whose lives had been turned around because they met Jesus while staying at the home; and about the eternal, spiritual fruit borne in all the countless lives Marcel touched while he was here with us. I was inspired to be of greater service in my own life, and reminded to be grateful for the contributions of those who have gone before.

We don't always get to see the fruit or personally reap the harvest of the seeds we sow, but rest assured: when you sow in faithfulness and obedience to God, there will be a harvest beyond your ability to imagine, that will reach into eternity.

Mom's Apple Pie

3 cups peeled and sliced apples
(Try "Granny Smith" for a tart pie,
and "Jonathan" for a sweeter pie)
1/2 cup sugar
1-1/2 tsp. cinnamon
One 8- or 9-inch unbaked pie crust

Combine sugar and cinnamon and pour over sliced apples. Let stand for ten minutes. Prepare topping.

Topping:
3/4 cup flour
1/2 cup sugar
1/3 cup butter

Mix topping ingredients together with fork. Place apple mixture in pie crust and sprinkle topping over it. Bake at 350° for one hour or until nicely browned. Serve warm with homemade vanilla ice cream for best results!

One of the fond childhood memories I share with my brother and sisters is that of an entire fall day spent in a local orchard with our grandparents, picking apples for eating, baking, and canning. We still make at least one excursion a year to "Apple-town," a charming country establishment a half hour from where we live. We always have a home-cooked lunch with hot apple dumplings for dessert, and we take home jars of apple butter and gallons of the best apple cider you ever tasted.

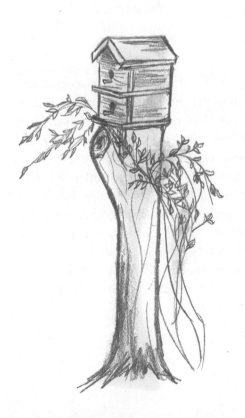

Believe the Best

> *Deacons, likewise, are to be men worthy of respect, sincere, not indulging in much wine, and not pursuing dishonest gain. They must keep hold of the deep truths of the faith with a clear conscience. They must first be tested; and then if there is nothing against them, let them serve as deacons. In the same way, their wives are to be women worthy of respect, not malicious talkers but temperate and trustworthy in everything.*
>
> 1 TIMOTHY 3:8–11

The last verse in this passage refers specifically to the wives of deacons in the church, but this principle applies to all of us. Not only should we not be malicious talkers, but we should also shun malicious talk. In fact, it should be very difficult to slander another brother or sister in my presence. I should be inclined not even to believe a bad report unless it is proved to be true. The truth is, many of us actually enjoy hearing and passing on a bad report, perhaps because we suddenly feel more holy by comparison, or vindicated in our own weakness. It is good to remember that when we slander our brother or sister, we slander Christ. In the flesh, most of us will enjoy a juicy bit of gossip. Only the Spirit of God can effectively guard our hearts and tongues and put this sin to death.

$\mathcal{I}$ doubt that mums got their name from keeping quiet. These boisterously colored flowers fairly shout out to be noticed and are synonymous with autumn. When choosing the perfect mums for your garden this fall, keep in mind that mums raised in nurseries specifically for outdoor planting flower better than those you would purchase at a florist. Mums from florists are usually intended for indoor decoration.

Letters from Christ

You yourselves are our letter, written on our hearts, known and read by everybody. You show that you are a letter from Christ, the result of our ministry, written not with ink but with the Spirit of the living God, not on tablets of stone but on tablets of human hearts.

2 CORINTHIANS 3:2–3

As Christians, and therefore, representatives of the Kingdom, we are walking test cases for His principles. Our actions have far-reaching and eternal consequences, not only in our own lives and in the lives of those close to us, but in the lives of more people than we can imagine—many more than we know or see personally in a day. When our actions are positive, the consequences are positive and sometimes glorious. That should be very encouraging and motivating. But if our actions are negative, then the results will be negative and sometimes tragic. And that should be very sobering. Our lives are meant to impact each other, since God's model for us has always been one of interdependence. We truly do not live in a spiritual vacuum.

Some annuals like zinnias and hollyhocks frequently reseed themselves, modeling the characteristics of perennials.

Delightful Inheritance

LORD, you have assigned me my portion and my cup; you have
made my lot secure. The boundary lines have fallen for me in
pleasant places; surely I have a delightful inheritance.

PSALM 16:5–6

I have always felt very blessed because I have a wonderful spiritual heritage. My dad, granddad, and great-grandfather, as well as many others in my extended family were ministers of the Gospel who lived what they preached. Not only did I grow up with a great example for my life, but I'm the recipient of the blessings God promises to the children of faithful men and women. If you have godly parents and grandparents, I hope you're grateful to them and to God. If you don't, please remember that when you become a Christian, the family of God becomes your family, and God becomes your Father. Old things pass away, all things become new. And your heritage as a child of God is the most beautiful of all. As a result, you are the one who can pass down a godly heritage to your children and your children's children. Then they will be blessed because of your faithfulness.

Many heirloom variety seeds of flowers and vegetables that are available today have been saved and passed down from generation to generation. The same beauty and flavor our grandparents enjoyed is available to us because they faithfully saved and replenished their seed supply.

Seventy Years Ago

Seventy years ago my father's mother's father
Led the clan of Nicholson
He and my great-grandmother had four lovely daughters
And a strong and honest son
And they traveled Arkansas and Oklahoma
Building arbors made of vine
And the people of the town would come at sundown
Some to scoff and some to see what they would find
And the sisters dressed in white
And the family sang and prayed into the night

And they rode in a covered wagon
As they walked in holiness
And they lived and preached the power and forgiveness
   of the Lord
Seventy years ago

Seventy years ago there wasn't much in preaching
But it never slowed them down
They loved the truth and all the hearts that He was reaching
And their eyes were on the crown

So they traveled Arkansas and Oklahoma
With a burning in their souls
And it drove them to their knees and to the next town
For the sake of a wealth they could not hold

And they rode in a covered wagon
As they walked in holiness
And they lived and preached the power and forgiveness
    of the Lord
Seventy years ago

Sometimes I feel like a pale reflection
Living in the blessing they passed down
Some of them have held me
Some never knew my name
But the secret has been found
I want to give this to my children
And when I am very old
I hope there still will be a story worth the telling
Of seventy years ago

"Seventy Years Ago" originally recorded on "Beyond a Dream" (Star Song Records) © 1993 Ariose Music/Mountain Spring Music—ASCAP.

Stage Fright

But he gives us more grace. That is why Scripture says: "God opposes the proud but gives grace to the humble." . . . Humble yourselves before the Lord, and he will lift you up.

JAMES 4:6, 10

When I was two years old I began to sing in church. At the age of six, I discovered stage fright and never sang in public again until I was a teenager. Even then I found it very difficult. At twenty, when I felt that God was calling me to a full-time music ministry, the issue was still not completely resolved, and it loomed as a significant hindrance.

At that point, my dad gave me some advice which still serves me well. "If you are God-conscious, you will not be self-conscious. If you will focus on the message God has called you to bring and on His heart for those listening, you will not have to worry about what anyone thinks of you." He knew that excessive self-awareness is actually a form of pride.

Pride is often the greatest source of all that is bad in our lives. It can reveal itself in so many ways, some subtle and some not-so-subtle. Pride causes us to be shy and insecure because we're so afraid of what others would think. It can keep us from even attempting to fulfill God's call on our lives for fear of failure. Or, it can take the form of independence and egotism. "I need no one. I can do this on my own, and I can do it better than anyone else." Whatever face it shows to the world, the end result of pride always separates us from others, from God's perfect plan for our lives, and worst of all from God Himself. The proud person will ultimately fail, either by throwing stones in his own path or by daring the Almighty to resist his efforts directly. But the humble person will inevitably succeed simply because God has promised to make sure he does.

The Shasta daisy is a humble perennial that is available with single or double flowers. Its old-fashioned charm and durability make it a perfect choice for cut arrangements.

Only One Life

Teach us to number our days aright, that we may gain a heart of wisdom. . . . May the favor of the Lord our God rest upon us; establish the work of our hands for us—yes, establish the work of our hands.

PSALM 90:12, 17

I first learned this passage in the form of a song. I was very young at the time and probably appreciated the music more than the message. Like most young people, even though I knew in my mind that my life on earth would have an end, I'm not sure I really believed it would ever come. Now, I find myself having reached the point where I have lived half my promised years. I want God to remind me daily that I'm not here forever so that I will set my priorities accordingly. I want the work of my hands to be established by God so that I may accomplish things that will really matter, not just for now in the eyes of men, but ten thousand years from now in the eyes of God. It is with good reason that many of our Christian grandmothers had this poem on their walls. "Only one life, 'twill soon be passed. Only what's done for Christ will last."

*K*nown for its cheerful appearance, the sunflower is an annual that is not merely one flower. Its center consists of more than two thousand tiny flowers that grow together!

$\mathcal{F}$or I will pour water on

the thirsty land, and streams

on the dry ground; I will pour

out my Spirit on your offspring,

and my blessing on your

descendants. They will spring up

like grass in a meadow, like

poplar trees by flowing streams.

ISAIAH 44:3–4

My Eyes Have Seen You

*Then Job replied to the LORD: "I know that you can do all things;
no plan of yours can be thwarted. You asked, 'Who is this that
obscures my counsel without knowledge?' Surely I spoke of things I
did not understand, things too wonderful for me to know. You said,
'Listen now, and I will speak; I will question you, and you shall
answer me.' My ears had heard of you, but now my eyes have seen
you. Therefore I despise myself and repent in dust and ashes."*

JOB 42:1–6

How can I believe that the Lord has anything but love for me? He has given me life, placed me in a world full of His wonder, and given me a spirit capable of communing with Him on the most intimate of levels. Like Job, I often look at my circumstances through the tiniest of pinholes and decide that I know what would be best for me in a particular situation. The Holy Spirit, the doubter's best friend, faithfully encourages us to look beyond our circumstances into the face of the Lord.

Most often, I see the perfect plan of the Lord as I look back, not around or ahead. It is then that I see His faultless wisdom at work in my life, bringing about the ultimate in His design for me. It is then that I fall on my knees and ask His forgiveness for allowing my blurred vision to dictate His position in my life.

Lord, please show me my unbelief so that I may repent and truly know You for who You really are—my only glory and the lifter of my head.

*D*id you know that God created a system that enables tulip bulbs, along with many seeds, to turn themselves root down when they are planted wrong side up? Yet another bit of encouraging evidence that proves, when everything seems out of control, God is not.

Speaking Life

The tongue has the power of life and death,
and those who love it will eat its fruit.
PROVERBS 18:21

The same tongue that can bring nourishment, healing, and life to a person's heart can also cut it into shreds in a moment. In choosing to regard others as more important than ourselves, we make great strides toward the goal the Lord has for us as brothers and sisters. Jesus tells us in Matthew 12:33 that a tree is identified by its fruit. Simply put, our words reflect our hearts. If we can learn to view our speech as an indicator of the condition of our hearts, we should be able to quickly recognize and determine the areas in our lives which are not yet fully yielded to the direction and Spirit of God.

Lord, in Your faithfulness to me and to those I influence, please show me clearly where my words do not reflect Your heart. Give me the grace to speak life to all those around me.

I recently learned that established strawberry plants send out new runners, or "shoots," each year. These runners form roots and may be cut off and transplanted to another location. You can have triple or more new strawberry plants the following year. I see this as yet another extraordinary display of God's creativity.

Johnson Grass

In the same way, count yourselves dead to sin but alive to God in Christ Jesus. Therefore do not let sin reign in your mortal body so that you obey its evil desires. Do not offer the parts of your body to sin, as instruments of wickedness, but rather offer yourselves to God, as those who have been brought from death to life; and offer the parts of your body to him as instruments of righteousness.

ROMANS 6:11–13

To many home owners, the words "Johnson grass" are synonymous with "distress" and "grief." Both my grandmothers waged a lifelong battle with Johnson grass. Through the years, gardeners have viewed this culprit as a true villain that threatens the life of the grasses they would love to have live in their yard. Johnson grass must be dug out by the roots—roots which not only grow down, but out!

An elder at my home fellowship once used Johnson grass as a metaphor to illustrate old sin that is allowed to remain in our lives. He is a retired farmer and testified to the fact that, "If Johnson grass is allowed to 'seed' or propagate instead of being dug out at first sighting, it is almost impossible to get rid of!" If we pull up only the visible signs of sin in our lives but do not allow the roots to be pulled, the magnitude of the consequences is often so far-reaching we don't even know how to begin "weeding." Of course, the Lord is faithful to forgive us when we repent, but allowing sin to remain in our life after the Holy Spirit first brings it to our attention is, in essence, agreeing to the far-reaching results of unconfessed sin.

137

Father, in Your love, please remind me that You always discipline out of love for me, and Your "weeding" in my life is always for my highest good.

Ornamental grasses are wonderful perennials whose roots offer protection against soil erosion. Their colors and textures offer dramatic beauty to any garden. Some taller grasses, such as the Goliath, make their own "music" when their leaves are blown by the wind.

Real Repentance

Seek the LORD while he may be found; call on him while he is near. Let the wicked forsake his way and the evil man his thoughts. Let him turn to the LORD, and he will have mercy on him, and to our God, for he will freely pardon.

ISAIAH 55:6–7

The Bible tells us that all have sinned. Even Christians are capable of making wrong choices. The important thing is how we respond to the sin in our lives. It's tempting to feel that our sin is so great that the Lord could never forgive us. It is equally tempting to simply forgive ourselves, with a silent reminder to never repeat the offense. Of course, neither of these is the appropriate response to sin in our lives. We must go to the Lord, admitting the break in our relationship. Then we must commit to Him our resolve to turn from our ways and return to His. It is only then that our repentance is real. It is not our place to rationalize or "write off" sin, which is any thought, act, or attitude that would grieve the Lord and be in contrast to His principles. Our place is at the foot of the cross, asking the Savior to once again cleanse us from our unrighteousness and restore us to close fellowship with Him.

Fountain of Grace

You have been faithful when I have been faithless
Oh, unending Fountain of Grace
Forever giving when I have been selfish
Oh, unending Fountain of Grace
Still the beginning of all that is holy
Unsearchable, Ancient of Days
I kneel before You and offer this vessel
Oh, unending Fountain of Grace

You were the constant when I chose to wander
Oh, unending Fountain of Grace
You were forgiveness when I cried for mercy
Oh, unending Fountain of Grace
You are the Author of all that is finished
I owe You my life and my praise
I kneel before You and offer this vessel
Oh, unending Fountain of Grace
Pour out the water of life on this vessel
Oh, unending Fountain of Grace

winter

$\mathcal{W}$inter is a time of rest, for both the gardener and the well-mulched garden. It is a season of renewal and rebirth, the time the Lord has designed to replenish the soil and refresh the mind and spirit of those who have been tilling it. Like a gardener's time of rest, the "winters" of a life are also filled with preparation and planning. Jeremiah 29:11 says, "'For I know the plans I have for you,' declares the LORD, 'plans to prosper you and not to harm you, plans to give you hope and a future.'" The certainty that the Lord delights in us is our peace. The temperature may drop and the snow may fall. But all the while we are snuggled up next to our heavenly Father, listening to His voice and dreaming His dreams with Him.

On Hold

> "The man with the two talents also came. 'Master,' he said,
> 'you entrusted me with two talents; see, I have gained two
> more.' His master replied, 'Well done, good and faithful servant!
> You have been faithful with a few things; I will put you in charge
> of many things. Come and share your master's happiness!'"
>
> MATTHEW 25:22–23

In the last few years I have talked with many people who feel like God has them "on hold." They are waiting for a real ministry to come along, and in the meantime, they are frustrated and discontented. It's hard to imagine that they are being very faithful in their current assignment. They see the opportunities before them as small and insignificant and therefore unimportant. Their attitude is that when God gives them an important job, then they will get excited and be faithful. What they don't realize is that God would never waste their time or His. He has placed them right where they are in order to prepare them for greater responsibility, and He is also watching to see if He can trust them with more authority. So those who are not willing to be faithful in little things actually delay their own progress toward their goals. God searches for hearts that are diligently and enthusiastically doing the next thing He gives them to do. And then He puts them in charge of more than they would have ever dreamed.

*S*ketching out new garden plans is a great winter evening activity that helps organize plantings and purchases for the next garden season. It's just the thing to keep our hearts and minds looking forward to the coming growth and beauty in the spring.

I Will Listen

Hard as it seems
Standing in dreams
Where is the dreamer now?
Wonder if I wanted to try
Would I remember how
I don't know the way to go from here
But I know that I have made my choice
And this is where I stand until He moves me on
And I will listen to His voice

This is the faith
Patience to wait
When there is nothing clear
Nothing to see
Still we believe
Jesus is very near
I cannot imagine what will come
But I've already made my choice
And this is where I stand until He moves me on
And I will listen to His voice

Could it be that He is only waiting there to see
If I will learn to love the dreams that He has dreamed for me
Can't imagine what the future holds
But I've already made my choice
And this is where I stand until He moves me on
And I will listen to His voice

"I Will Listen" originally recorded on "Where I Stand" (Sparrow Records) ©
1996 Ariose Music/Mountain Spring Music—ASCAP.

Running to the Rescue

He reached down from on high and took hold of me; he drew me out of deep waters. He rescued me from my powerful enemy, from my foes, who were too strong for me. They confronted me in the day of my disaster, but the LORD was my support.

PSALM 18:16–19

Several years ago, the Lord used this psalm to minister great hope to me during a particularly difficult time in my life. Verses 1–15 tell us about David's life-threatening circumstances, his cry to the Lord for help, and God's response. This is the great part! It takes nine whole verses to describe, in detail, not only the lightning speed with which God rushed to the aid of a faithful child in danger, but also His intense anger directed at those who would dare to harm that child. In other words, He responded exactly the way you would expect a father to respond if someone was threatening his child. If you have been tempted to wonder whether or not God hears you when you cry to Him for help, or whether He even cares, sit down and read Psalm 18 all the way through and put yourself in David's place. God does rescue His children—because He delights in us.

Running to the Rescue

Listening every time you cry
He delights in you
Scattering evil left and right
Just to get you through

Running to the rescue
He will come to save you
Righteous anger flaming
Little child reclaiming

"Running to the Rescue" originally recorded on "Same Girl" (Star Song Records) © 1987 StraightWay Music/Mountain Spring Music—ASCAP.

I found it very interesting to learn that small figs in a very warm climate can "overwinter" and ripen to mature fruit in the next season. This is yet another shining example of God's true resourcefulness. Since He put that much thought into the growth pattern of a fig, just imagine what He has in store for the children He loves so much.

Hope in You

Some trust in chariots and some in horses, but we trust in the name of the LORD our God.

PSALM 20:7

Recently I visited Honduras with a team from World Vision, a wonderful organization that helps to feed hungry children around the world. I went to meet the little boy I sponsor and to see, firsthand, the need and the progress there. We spent the first day in a remote village at the top of a mountain. As evening approached, a torrential rain set in. Before we could begin our journey down the mountain to reach the main highway, we first had to climb a small hill. The narrow dirt road had turned to very slippery mud, and our tough, "go anywhere" vehicle was going absolutely nowhere!

The solution to our problem finally appeared in the form of a team of oxen, owned by a local farmer. They were hitched to the front of our vehicle and promptly pulled it to the top of the hill. We all had a good laugh over the irony of the situation. After thousands of years of development, man's best efforts to create efficient, all-terrain transportation couldn't compete with one of God's original designs.

As I continued to reflect, the day's events also served as a reminder of an even more fundamental lesson. Whatever form it may take, ultimately the solution to any problem always comes from God. I believe He gives us tools to work with: systems, partners, helpers, and financial provision. But it seems so easy for Christians to transfer their faith from God to tangible and visible resources. I've found that I need to remind myself very often that only God is capable of being my salvation in any given circumstance. He is the only One who is always faithful—incapable of letting me down. Whenever we foolishly put our faith in chariots and horses (or four-wheel drive vehicles and oxen), we will always live to regret it. But for those whose trust is in the name of the Lord, there is no regret. Trust in Him is always rewarded with faithfulness.

Hope in You

I will find my hope in You
Trusting in no man
Leaning not to earthly wisdom
Things I understand

Hide my heart away
Fill me with Your mind
Let the world forsake me
I will find my hope in You

For a quick pick-me-up, a cup of chamomile tea and a few minutes alone with the Lord can do wonders! Just steep a chamomile tea bag in hot water for about ten minutes. While you're waiting, choose a favorite soothing tape or CD and light a scented candle. (During cool weather, try a spicy cinnamon scent. In warmer weather, gardenia is perfect.) Pour a cup of tea, sit in a comfy chair, and reflect on the goodness of the Lord to you personally. A few moments of solitude with the Lord will be sure to invigorate you, spiritually and physically. Note: for a warm weather treat, try iced raspberry tea.

*A*s long as the earth endures,

seedtime and harvest,

cold and heat,

summer and winter,

day and night

will never cease."

GENESIS 8:22

Treasures in Heaven

> "Do not store up for yourselves treasures on earth, where moth
> and rust destroy, and where thieves break in and steal. But store
> up for yourselves treasures in heaven, where moth and rust do
> not destroy, and where thieves do not break in and steal. For
> where your treasure is, there your heart will be also."
>
> MATTHEW 6:19

*A*mong the wonderful qualities of the older home we recently purchased was the beautiful flower garden immediately beyond the sunroom windows at the back of the house. However, there were other discoveries that were not so wonderful, and a good deal of work had to be done before we could move in. During the renovation we were visited by burglars, who managed to completely demolish the back doors. Around the time we finally did move in, the city began work widening the street in front of our house. This seemed like a good thing until the crew working on the street severed our main plumbing line, evidenced by things that belong in the yard beginning to overflow into the basement. "That's okay," we thought, "we can handle this." And another crew came to install a new plumbing line.

Previous owners had put in an underground sprinkler system, and somehow the new crew severed irrigation lines all over the yard. So, yet another crew came to fix that. At this point, we had geysers everywhere and the yard was completely devastated. There was no grass—only big holes and piles of dirt. Our front lawn looked like downtown Beirut!

The low point for me came when I returned home from a tour which had lasted throughout the fall. I was looking forward to putting up my Christmas tree, sitting in front of the fire, listening to Bing Crosby, and eating cookies. My husband picked me up at the airport and informed me that we would be staying in a hotel because we had no plumbing, no water, and no electricity. I dissolved into a puddle of tears. Very grown-up, very mature—very embarrassing in retrospect. Of course all these things seemed huge to me at the time—but they weren't. They were very small.

All of us have possessions that are blessings from God. It's fine to enjoy them, but we should never let them occupy too high a place in our hearts. Temporal treasures by nature are subject to theft and deterioration. This may seem like a negative, but in reality the day-to-day aggravations we encounter give us the wonderful opportunity to once again set our affections on Him—to store up our treasures in heaven.

Fix Your Eyes

When I look into Your eyes
I see the love that died for me
When I look into Your eyes
I see the hope that I will be a faithful child
Following close behind
Following ever blinded
To the things that should not move me
Saying to my soul
Fix your eyes on Jesus
When I look into Your eyes
I feel the grief when I have sinned
When I look into Your eyes
I find delight when I have been a faithful child
Following close behind
Following ever blinded
To the things that should not move me
Saying to my soul
Fix your eyes on Jesus
Fix your eyes upon the prize
The highest calling you will find
Following close behind
Following ever blinded
To the things that should not move me
Saying to my soul
Fix your eyes on Jesus

"Fix Your Eyes" originally recorded on "Cry for the Desert" (Star Song Records) © 1990 Ariose Music/Mountain Spring Music—ASCAP.

The Lord Is My Shepherd

The LORD is my shepherd, I shall not be in want. He makes me lie down in green pastures, he leads me beside quiet waters, he restores my soul. He guides me in paths of righteousness for his name's sake. Even though I walk through the valley of the shadow of death, I will fear no evil, for you are with me; your rod and your staff, they comfort me. You prepare a table before me in the presence of my enemies. You anoint my head with oil; my cup overflows. Surely goodness and love will follow me all the days of my life, and I will dwell in the house of the LORD forever.

PSALM 23

God has such a tender heart toward each of His children. He truly cares about the stresses and painful circumstances in our lives. No matter how busy we are we must give Him the time to lead us beside still waters and anoint our heads with oil, because only He can restore a tired and hurting soul.

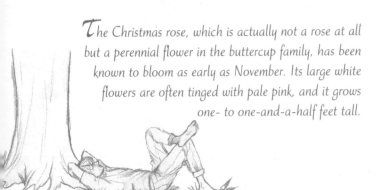

The Christmas rose, which is actually not a rose at all but a perennial flower in the buttercup family, has been known to bloom as early as November. Its large white flowers are often tinged with pale pink, and it grows one- to one-and-a-half feet tall.

Living Sacrifice

Therefore, I urge you, brothers, in view of God's mercy, to offer your bodies as living sacrifices, holy and pleasing to God—this is your spiritual act of worship.

ROMANS 12:1

One day a few years ago, Jack and I were talking with my dad about some of the struggles and challenges we were facing. Jack, who is very compassionate by nature, made the comment, "Twila really pays a price to do what she does." At the time, I had been away from home a lot; I was really tired and, honestly, feeling just a little sorry for myself. I remember thinking, *You know, that's right. I really do.*

My dad responded out loud, "That's true. She does. So do all of us who are obedient to the call of God. But none of us pay anywhere near the price Jesus paid when He died for us on the cross."

The issue was settled . . . permanently.

Lamb of God

Your only Son, no sin to hide
But You have sent Him from Your side
To walk upon this guilty sod
And to become the Lamb of God
Your gift of love they crucified
They laughed and scorned Him as He died

The humble King they named a fraud
And sacrificed the Lamb of God

Oh Lamb of God, sweet Lamb of God
I love the Holy Lamb of God
Oh wash me in His precious blood
My Jesus Christ the Lamb of God

I was so lost I should have died
But You have brought me to Your side
To be led by Your staff and rod
And to be called a lamb of God

Oh Lamb of God, sweet Lamb of God
I love the Holy Lamb of God
Oh wash me in His precious blood
Till I am just a lamb of God
Oh wash me in His precious blood
My Jesus Christ the Lamb of God

Let the Little Children Come

Jesus said, "Let the little children come to me, and do not hinder
them, for the kingdom of heaven belongs to such as these."

MATTHEW 19:14

*M*y friend Debbie has five children and is a wonderful
mother. She's always looking for opportunities to teach
God's love and truth by word and by example. A few years ago
at Christmastime, her daily route took her and the children by
a local church where a large nativity scene was prominently displayed. My friend immediately saw this as a beautiful way to
illustrate the story of Christmas for her youngest daughter, Carly,
who was almost three years old at the time. Debbie shared how
God loved us all so much that He sent His only Son to earth to
save us from the wrong we had done—that the little baby Jesus
lying in the manger was also God Himself and that we could
know Him and love Him in return. Carly was enthralled with
this information, and every day as they passed the nativity scene
she would comment on the nearness of God.

One day, early in the new year, they were driving past the
church when Carly suddenly burst into tears. Afraid Carly had
been hurt somehow, Debbie asked, "Honey, what's wrong?"

Through her sobs, the child answered, "Mommy, God is
gone!"

Sure enough, the season having passed, the nativity scene had
been dismantled and God did indeed appear to be gone. Of
course, this "misunderstanding" inspired a discussion of the fact
that God is really a spirit and can actually live all the time in

our hearts. It also inspired the adults who later heard the story to ask ourselves, "Wouldn't it be wonderful if we were all so acutely aware of our desperate need for the constant presence of God in our lives?"

It's the Thought

And a loving thought sends us out to find
Something special for someone on our mind
And we think of friends and our family
As we hang our gifts on the Christmas tree

It's the thought that counts when the thought is love
It's the thought that counts when you're thinking of
How the money flows in vast amounts
When the thought is love it's the thought that counts

And a loving thought sent a snow white lamb
To a little town known as Bethlehem
And the little lamb thought of you and me
As He hung His gift on the Christmas tree

It's the thought that counts when the thought is love
It's the thought that counts when you're thinking of
All the blood that flowed in vast amounts
When the thought is love it's the thought that counts

Think of the precious gift He gave
Think of the life He thought to save

And the blood that flowed in vast amounts
When the thought is love it's the thought that counts

God's House

I will praise the LORD, who counsels me; even at night my heart instructs me. I have set the LORD always before me. Because he is at my right hand, I will not be shaken.

PSALM 16:7–8

When I read this passage I picture myself actually living with God in the same house, talking with Him during the day, listening to His wise counsel. As He speaks with me He ministers comfort, encouragement, and correction, even in my sleep. If I am always aware of the very real and close presence of God, I will not be swayed by the pressures of life, regardless of my natural inclinations. God's firm yet loving hand will gently take hold of mine and keep me steady. There's nothing sweeter and more secure than the picture of a father holding his child's hand as they walk. God wants to be just like that father to us.

Paper whites are a favorite accent in our home. Their sweet fragrance adds festivity to the Christmas season of joy and celebration. Paper whites are easily forced (making bulbs bloom early) in 3–5 weeks by placing in a shallow container of gravel and keeping the roots covered with water. Keep in a dimly lit area until they have bloomed, then place near a sunny window. You can tie fabric bows around their beautiful stems to add even more holiday charm.

More Precious Than Gold

The law of the LORD is perfect, reviving the soul. The statutes of the LORD are trustworthy, making wise the simple. The precepts of the LORD are right, giving joy to the heart. The commands of the LORD are radiant, giving light to the eyes. The fear of the LORD is pure, enduring forever. The ordinances of the LORD are sure and altogether righteous. They are more precious than gold, than much pure gold; they are sweeter than honey, than honey from the comb. By them is your servant warned; in keeping them there is great reward.

PSALM 19:7–11

We should never underestimate the value of God's principles. They are literally treasures that He has given us. If we fail to hold dear His truth, if we seek first after gold and other earthly treasures, we will be continually frustrated, discontented, and even brokenhearted. But if we will obey His laws, listen to His words, heed His warnings, and follow His guidelines, they will always be a source of great joy in our lives. And we will be truly fulfilled.

$\mathcal{M}$any seed catalogs are shipped to eager gardeners in February. These catalogs are a great resource for obtaining particular varieties you may have been wanting to try (or new varieties you want to discover). Most catalogs are free or very reasonably priced (we know of one company that requests ten stamps or a box of chocolates)! They usually include plant histories and specific planting instructions. But be forewarned: you may have a tendency to get carried away, ordering more than just a few samples of the amazing variety our Father has lovingly supplied.

Tootsie Rolls

"For God so loved the world that he gave his one and only Son, that whoever believes in him shall not perish but have eternal life."

JOHN 3:16

They tell me I was a fairly compliant child—that disapproval was generally as effective a discipline as spanking. Generally—but not always. There certainly were occasions when I was willfully disobedient.

One of those occasions stands out in my memory—not because of what I did—I honestly don't remember. It's my dad's response I will never forget.

I was about five years old, and we must have been out together as a family when I committed my offense, because I remember being promised a spanking when we got home. Upon our arrival, I was not immediately punished, and I began to nurse a childish hope that Dad would forget. I even tried bringing up other interesting topics of conversation in an effort to further distract him from his purpose. Of course it didn't work. He had never forgotten—even for a moment.

After some time, he finally called my name. "Twila, come with me—we're going for a ride in the car." I was puzzled but followed quietly. We drove to a nearby grocery store where, once inside, he led me straight to the candy aisle and told me to choose my favorite candy. Despite a growing concern for my father's mental state, I managed to select a large bag of Tootsie Rolls.

By the time we got back home, I was fairly bursting with curiosity. Dad simply sat down in a chair on the front porch and motioned for me to climb up on his lap.

As I sat there, eating one Tootsie Roll after another, he told me again a story I had heard many times before. He said that everyone in the world had sinned and deserved to be punished. But God had sent His only Son, Jesus, to die on a cross, so that instead of being punished, we could all be given the gift of eternal life. In just the same way, I had been given the gift of Tootsie Rolls instead of the painful consequences I had earned.

In case you're wondering, most of the spankings I was promised in my life were actually delivered. But on this day, my dad took the time to paint a beautiful picture of God's mercy and grace for a disobedient child.

At the time, I thought my dad's gift was a bag of Tootsie Rolls. Now I know better.

The chocolate cosmos is a flower I want to know more about. This incredible blossom actually smells like chocolate! What more needs to be said?

*O*kay . . . I know this has absolutely nothing to do with anything spiritual or botanical. These just happen to be my favorite cookies in the whole world, and I want to share them with you. (Actually, someone did have to grow the oats, didn't they?)

Angie's Oatmeal Chocolate Chip Cookies

1 cup shortening
1-1/4 cups firmly packed brown sugar
1/2 cup granulated sugar
2 eggs
2 tbsp. milk
2 tsp. vanilla
1-3/4 cups all-purpose flour
1 tsp. baking soda
1/2 teaspoon salt (optional)
2-1/2 cups uncooked oats
1 cup semi-sweet chocolate pieces

Preheat oven to 375°. Beat together shortening and sugars until creamy. Add eggs, milk, and vanilla; beat well. Add combined flour, baking soda, and salt; mix well. Stir in oats, chocolate pieces, and nuts; mix well. Drop by heaping tablespoons onto ungreased cookie sheet. Bake 8 to 9 minutes. Cool 1 minute on cookie sheet; remove to wire rack.

The Greatest Gifts

Therefore, since we have been justified through faith, we have peace
with God through our Lord Jesus Christ, through whom we have
gained access by faith into this grace in which we now stand. And
we rejoice in the hope of the glory of God. Not only so, but we also
rejoice in our sufferings, because we know that suffering produces
perseverance; perseverance, character; and character, hope. And
hope does not disappoint us, because God has poured out his love
into our hearts by the Holy Spirit, whom he has given us.

ROMANS 5:1–5

I have to admit that the Scriptures regarding suffering have never been my favorites. I have seen God working in other people's lives through their suffering, but I always kind of hoped that I would be an exception—that I could learn the things I needed to learn just by hearing them and reading about them. However, it doesn't work that way. In spite of my careful maneuvering, I walked right into the painful side of God's loving plan for me. Just as I suspected, I did not enjoy it. If I had, it wouldn't have been suffering. But like millions of my brothers and sisters, as I look back on my life so far, I recognize that the greatest gifts and the deepest foundations in my life have been the results of those circumstances I would have never chosen.

Father, please give me wisdom to quickly embrace Your will for my
life—whatever it is.

This Thorn

Thank You for this thorn embedded in my flesh
I can feel the mystery; my spirit is made fresh
You are sovereign still and forever wise
I can see the miracle opening my eyes
To a proud heart so quick to judge
Laying down crosses and carrying grudges
The veil has been torn
And I thank You for this thorn

Thank You for this thorn; fellowship of pain
Teaching me to know You more; never to complain
Thank You for this love planted in my side
Faithful, patient miracle opening my eyes

I never thought I'd say it without reservation
But I am truly grateful for this piercing revelation
Of a proud heart so quick to judge
Laying down crosses and carrying grudges
The veil has been torn
And I thank You for this thorn

And if You choose to take it I will praise You
And thank You for the healing in Your name
But if it must remain I thank You for Your rod
Evidence of Father-love for a child of God

I join You in the sorrow
So much less than You have borne
And I thank you
Really, I thank You
Lord, I thank You
I thank You for this thorn

Miracles and Grace

> *But he said to me, "My grace is sufficient for you, for my power is made perfect in weakness." Therefore I will boast all the more gladly about my weaknesses, so that Christ's power may rest on me. That is why, for Christ's sake, I delight in weaknesses, in insults, in hardships, in persecutions, in difficulties. For when I am weak, then I am strong.*
>
> 2 CORINTHIANS 12:9–10

When I was fifteen years old, I read *The Hiding Place* by Corrie ten Boom. She told how her father had illustrated the perfect timing of God's grace when she was a little girl. "Corrie, when we go on a trip, when do I give you your train ticket?... Just before we get on the train—not too early, not too late— just when you need it! God's grace is like that. When He allows you to walk through a difficult circumstance, that's when He gives you the grace—just when you need it!" This advice had a great impact on Corrie, and of course Corrie had a great impact on millions of people, including a teenage girl who wondered if that grace would really be enough when God allowed her to face difficult circumstances.

Four years later, at the age of nineteen, I needed my first megadose of God's grace. My father had been invited to teach in Europe, and Mom really wanted to go with him, but her mother was ill and we were caring for her in our home. And then there were the "kids": Starla, eleven; Oren, ten; and Angie, seven. At the time, I was attending the YWAM School of Evangelism in Arkansas. Our mornings and evenings were full, but we had afternoons off, and I thought I could handle school, housework, Grandma, and the kids for three weeks. I said, "Mom, go with Dad! It's only three weeks—I can do this! No problem!"

So she went, and everything was okay—until one night just a few days before my parents were due home. My aunt called to tell me that Mom and Dad had been in a terrible car accident in Germany. They were both critically injured, and Dad would be in the hospital for at least two months; Mom, too—if she lived. She was in a coma, and the doctors really didn't expect her to survive. People all over the world began to pray for my parents. I didn't know how to tell my very sick grandmother that her only daughter was fighting for her life thousands of miles away.

A few nights later my other grandmother, who lived next door, rang the bell at 3:00 A.M. "Twila, come quickly! Your grandfather's dying!" As I threw on my clothes, my heart pounded wildly. I didn't know if I would ever see my parents again. I was responsible for a sick grandmother and three children. And now this? I looked toward heaven and moaned, "Lord, what next?" I was at the very end of my ability to cope—and that's when God literally poured out His grace—just enough, just in time!

Grandpa did not die that night. He recovered from his heart attack, and I began to discover what it meant to walk in supernatural strength. There were difficult days and days when I needed forgiveness more than anything else. But the grace was always there, and whenever I accepted it, I really was okay! God really wouldn't put more on me than I could bear—in His strength. Nobody could believe how well I was doing!

After a month, Mom awakened from the coma—just in time for Easter! My best friend took care of the household, Grandma, and the kids for a week, and my uncle and I flew to Germany to see my parents for the first time since the accident. And only another month after that, Mom and Dad were able to leave the hospital and return home. Today they are fully recovered with only a few small, physical reminders that they are walking miracles!

There have been many times since I was nineteen that I have needed the grace to do what I ought to do. Many times I have accepted that grace, and sadly, sometimes I haven't. But I have never again wondered if it was really there.

preservation

One of my grandmother's favorite summertime activities was canning. Her pantry was always brimming with jars of preserves, juices, relishes, and vegetables, all beautifully displaying her handiwork, perfected over many years. To Grandma, canning was an art. She valued not only the result, but the process as well. The journals of her life also reflected this philosophy. She understood that documenting the work of the Lord in her life was an important aspect of its preservation.

The following pages have been added as an encouragement for you to begin, maybe for the first time, journaling the paths you have walked and are walking with the Lord. This record serves to remind us of lessons learned. It is also a means of personally honoring the One who created and preserves us, body, soul, and spirit.

$\mathcal{S}$tarla cans chow-chow relish in the tradition our grandmother began before we were born. Chow-chow is a green tomato relish that is the perfect accompaniment to pinto beans and corn bread on a chilly night. It's also great on hot dogs and, well, pretty much anything!

Chow-Chow Relish

1 quart chopped cabbage (about 1 small head)
2 cups chopped green tomatoes (about 4 medium)
2 cups chopped onions (about 2 medium)
2 cups chopped sweet green peppers (about 4 small)
1 cup chopped sweet red peppers (about 2 small)
3 tablespoons salt
1-1/2 cups sugar
2 tsp. celery seed
2 tsp. dry mustard
1 tsp. mustard seed
1 tsp. turmeric
1/2 tsp. ginger
2-1/2 cups vinegar

Combine chopped vegetables; sprinkle with salt. Let stand 4 to 6 hours in a cool place. Drain well.

Combine vinegar, sugar, and spices in large sauce pot. Simmer 10 minutes. Add vegetables; simmer 10 minutes. Bring to a boil.

Pack hot into hot jars, leaving 1/4-inch headspace. (Use only clean canning jars with lids and new seals. Follow all manufacturer's directions.) Adjust caps. Process 10 minutes in boiling water bath. Yield: about 4 pints.

Many herbs can be frozen straight from the garden for winter soups and casseroles. Wash, drain, and pat dry the herbs, then place them in bunches in small freezer bags. Be sure to seal and label each bag carefully. When needed, simply snip frozen herbs with scissors.

"I am the true vine, and my Father is the gardener."
—John 15:1

From the fruit of his mouth a man's stomach is filled; with the harvest from his lips he is satisfied. — Proverbs 18:20

He who gathers crops in summer is a wise son, but he who sleeps during a harvest is a disgraceful son. — Proverbs 10:5

"'Until now, the vine and the fig tree, the pomegranate and the olive tree have not borne fruit. From this day on I will bless you.'" — Haggai 2:19

"Six days you shall labor, but on the seventh day you shall rest; even during the plowing season and harvest you must rest." — Exodus 34:21

"But the seed on good soil stands for those with a
noble and good heart, who hear the word, retain it,
and by persevering produce a crop." — Luke 8:15

They sowed fields and planted vineyards that yielded a fruitful harvest; he blessed them, and their numbers greatly increased, and he did not let their herds diminish. — Psalm 107:37–38

"Remain in me, and I will remain in you. No branch can bear fruit by itself; it must remain in the vine. Neither can you bear fruit unless you remain in me." —John 15:4

You care for the land and water it; you enrich it abundantly.
The streams of God are filled with water to provide the people
with grain, for so you have ordained it. — Psalm 65:9

"So I gave you a land on which you did not toil and cities you did not build; and you live in them and eat from vineyards and olive groves that you did not plant." —Joshua 24:13

He who works his land will have abundant food, but the one who chases fantasies will have his fill of poverty.
— Proverbs 28:19

Blessed are all who fear the LORD, who walk in his ways. You will eat the fruit of your labor; blessings and prosperity will be yours. — Psalm 128:1–2

The righteous will never be uprooted, but the wicked will not remain in the land. — Proverbs 10:30

"Yet he has not left himself without testimony: He has shown kindness by giving you rain from heaven and crops in their seasons; he provides you with plenty of food and fills your hearts with joy." — Acts 14:17

He replied, "If you have faith as small as a mustard seed, you can say to this mulberry tree, 'Be uprooted and planted in the sea,' and it will obey you." — Luke 17:6

"The seed will grow well, the vine will yield its fruit,
the ground will produce its crops, and the heavens will drop
their dew. I will give all these things as an inheritance to the
remnant of this people." —Zechariah 8:12

World Vision

*Remember this: Whoever sows sparingly will also reap sparingly,
and whoever sows generously will also reap generously.*

2 CORINTHIANS 9:6

There is a special place in my heart for the ministry of World
Vision. As I have often said, "They do the practical work of
God's mercy, around the world, on our behalf." I believe we are
all very aware of the severe needs for food, clean water, health
care, and education in so many places, and I believe we truly want
to help. The thing that so encourages me about World Vision is
the fact that I have personally seen the vast, immediate, and

permanent difference they make in a community, in a family, and in the life of a single child.

For just $22* a month, you and your family can be a part of this wonderful chain of love. When you sponsor a child you actually become an important part of his life, and he becomes a part of yours. Even if you never have the chance to meet your sponsored child personally on this earth, there is an eternal bond formed between you—because God has allowed you to help change his destiny!

For me, being a World Vision sponsor is not just a responsibility; it's an honor—one I encourage you to share.

To sponsor children please write:

World Vision Child Sponsorship
P.O. Box 70050
Tacoma, WA 98481-0050
(800) 444–2522

*as of 1998

Youth With A Mission

> He told them, "The harvest is plentiful, but the workers
> are few. Ask the Lord of the harvest, therefore, to
> send out workers into his harvest field."
>
> LUKE 10:2

You may have noticed several references to Youth With A Mission throughout this book. That's because it is my home fellowship and a very large part of who I am. I grew up there and I am "sent out" from there in ministry. These are the people who support me in prayer and help to keep me focused and accountable.

Years ago, I attended the Discipleship Training School and the School of Evangelism, which I consider to be foundational in my life and ministry. I have also had the privilege of taking part in missionary outreaches with YWAM.

The fact that I have had such an up close view of this organization over the years has only served to increase my admiration for the work that is done and for the people who do it.

There is nothing special about this group except that they are committed and available to the Lord. Anyone can be a part of the ministry of Youth With A Mission. There are opportunities for both long- and short-term missionary service, and for training at all levels, including a four-year college with a missions perspective.

If reading this book has inspired you to learn more, please write to:

Youth With A Mission
P.O. Box 7
Elm Springs, AR 72728-0007
Phone: (800) 735–YWAM (9926)
Fax: (501) 248–1455
E-mail Address: 74604,3336@Compuserve

Twila Paris Discography

Perennial—Songs for the Seasons of Life	1998	Sparrow
Where I Stand	1996	Sparrow
The Time Is Now*	1995	Star Song
Beyond a Dream	1994	Star Song
A Heart That Knows You	1992	Star Song
Sanctuary	1991	Star Song
Early Works	1990	Benson
Cry for the Desert	1990	Star Song
It's the Thought	1989	Star Song
For Every Heart	1988	Star Song
Same Girl	1987	Star Song
Kingdom Seekers	1986	Star Song
The Best of Twila Paris	1985	Milk & Honey
The Warrior Is a Child	1984	Milk & Honey
Keepin' My Eyes on You	1982	Milk & Honey
Knowin' You're Around	1981	Milk & Honey

*Four-song compilation CD

*T*wila Paris has been honored three years in a row as the Gospel Music Association's Female Vocalist of the Year. With fourteen albums to her credit, she has written all twenty-five of her number-one radio singles. She is coauthor with Robert Webber of *In This Sanctuary*. She and her husband, Jack, live in Fayetteville, Arkansas.

*S*tarla Paris Novak and her husband, Mike, live in Elm Springs, Arkansas, where they serve in leadership at Youth With A Mission. Starla is a gifted homemaker with a special flair for cooking, gardening, entertaining, and finding bargains. She has also toured with Twila for the past several years singing background vocals.

*A*ngie Paris has worked full-time with Youth With A Mission for the past seven years. She has participated in many foreign outreaches, beginning with summer mission trips as a young teenager. Angie is a musician as well as an artist, and has just finished writing and recording her first album.